MIKE'S
UNFORGETTABLE ST. LOUIS HISTORY
VOLUME 1

MIKE KLECKNER

Mike's Unforgettable St. Louis History, Volume 1
© Mike Kleckner, 2021

To learn more about Mike's Unforgettable St. Louis History books, visit
MikesUnforgettableStLouis.com.

This book was edited, designed, laid out, proofread, and publicized by an
Editwright team. Visit editwright.com to learn more about Editwright's work.

Developmental editing by Andrew Doty
Copyediting by Lisa Ashpole
Paperback design and layout by Peggy Nehmen, n-kcreative.com
Proofreading by Karen L. Tucker
Indexed by Linda Presto

Published by Kleck, LLC

Typeset in Meta Pro, Meta Serif Pro, Pintanina, and Les Paul

First Printing: 2021

ISBN 978-1-7371607-0-0 (Paperback)
ISBN 978-1-7371607-1-7 (E-book)
BISAC: HIS036090: HISTORY / United States / State & Local / Midwest

On the cover, left to right: Missouri River Steamboats, taken from a painting by
Oscar E. Berninghaus (page 172); Adelaide Neilson, *J., Gurney & Son, Publisher*
(page 182); Union Station, *published by The St. Louis News Company* (page 55).
Back cover: Thomas J. Hicks, winner of Marathon Race, *photograph by Charles J. P.
Lucas* (page 187).

DEDICATION

To my mother, Robin, for passing on to me
my love of reading, writing, and history;
to my wife, Christine, for her incredible patience
and support of my passions and hobbies;
to my children, Teddy and Josie,
for inspiring me to be a better person.

President Theodore Roosevelt and aviator Archibald Hoxsey
in St. Louis (page 191). Photograph by Bain News Service.

CONTENTS

ABOUT THiS BOOK

For most of my adult life, I have cut out, collected, and organized any article that included an interesting fact or story about St. Louis history. The publications I read regularly are the *St. Louis Post-Dispatch*, *Webster-Kirkwood Times*, *West Newsmagazine*, *Town&Style*, *Ladue News*, *Chesterfield Lifestyle*, *Kirkwood Lifestyle*, *Chesterfield Out & About*, *stlzoo*, and *AAA Midwest Traveler*. The clippings have included obituaries, real estate listings, op-eds, and other articles that focused on a particular notable person, building, or area in St. Louis. I have always been a thorough and in-depth reader. I get most excited when I find that one unique, interesting St. Louis history fact that is buried deep within something like a promo about a new real estate development.

Over time, I decided to turn all of the content I collected into a book. I want this book to serve as a quick reference, easy reading, and fun St. Louis history book.

In order to stay true to my original concept for the book, the content I included has been sourced solely from the clippings I collected. That being said, some sections may leave you wanting more. But my ultimate goal is for this book to spark your curiosity. My hope is that this collage of stories will do just that. If you get a sudden desire to do your own research to learn more about a certain individual or house, then I will consider this book a success.

This book includes some rare, unique, quirky, and mostly unknown facts and stories about St. Louis. I love to learn new things, so my reading and collecting won't stop.

If you have a fun and unique story to share, please do not hesitate to reach out. I love talking St. Louis!

BUILDINGS

My curiosity and passion for St. Louis history all started with the city's beautiful historic mansions. From attending guided tours of mansions in the Central West End with my mom to bugging my wife every time we walk by a three-story stone house in Lafayette Square, historic homes were the first to win my heart. When exploring St. Louis, you may be surprised at the number of large, stately mansions. But when you remember that St. Louis is truly an old-money city built on fur trading, beer, tobacco, and shoes, you realize how many founding fathers and prominent barons built homes here.

I get sad when I hear about historic homes being demolished for new development. Preserving historic homes is very important to me. I often wish I could have seen the private street of Vandeventer Place, of which old photographs show homes that make some of the Central West End mansions seem small. I am lucky that I can still enjoy some of the amazing homes in Lafayette Square, Compton Heights, the Central West End, Kirkwood, Clayton, etc. Want to explore a little-known gem? Check out Visitation Park in North City.

One of the most magical properties in the area, and one on which I have actually never set foot, is the Hunter Farms estate in Chesterfield. There are two mansions on the property, each over 13,500 square feet, in addition to several other houses and structures. You can catch a glimpse of the 300+ acre property as you are driving east on Ladue Road (from 141). At nighttime, you can see the lights that surround the body of water on the property. President George W. Bush was known to stay at one of the houses on the property when he visited St. Louis. Legend has it that kids try to sneak into the property to fish in the pond.

More recently, I did some exploring of a neat, private property in the village of Huntleigh. While driving on Geyer heading toward Kirkwood, I noticed a sprawling piece of property that was being partially developed. After doing some digging, I found out that the property was originally over 50 acres and was owned by the Orthwein family, prominent in their own right and descendants of the Busch family. The equestrian property included a beautiful mansion of more than 11,500 square feet plus several riding trails and horse stables. The house was later owned by the Schnucks family and, more recently, Marc Bulger, the former St. Louis Rams quarterback. Part of the land was recently sold, and a new house is being built on the site, but the original Orthwein mansion remains.

The commercial architecture in St. Louis is special too. I love exploring downtown streets like Washington Avenue and other streets around Busch Stadium. If you look closely enough at some of the old buildings, you will likely see the slightly faded name of the company that used to be housed in that building. Several of the names reflect shoe, tobacco, and paper companies.

The following are some of the houses and buildings that interest me as a result of their architecture, original owner, history, or grandeur.

COMMERCIAL

....

St. Louis Psychiatric Rehabilitation Center

The St. Louis Psychiatric Rehabilitation Center, formerly known as the St. Louis County Lunatic Asylum, opened in 1869 with 127 patients. The land it sits on was considered countryside at that time, with nearby Tower Grove Park still in the planning phase. Henry Shaw, the founder of Tower Grove Park, donated more than 200 shade trees to be planted on the grounds. The building sits on the highest point in St. Louis, on Arsenal Street.

The building, an important piece of architecture and a symbol of the spirit of St. Louis, was designed by William Rumbold. Rumbold was a local architect who designed the Old Courthouse in downtown St. Louis and consulted on the design of the U.S. Capitol building.

In the late 1800s, superintendent Edward Runge and his wife would host patients in their apartment for "social evenings" where they would recite poetry and listen to music.

A round room in the basement included a turntable for hand-powered railcars to transport trays of food and supplies. A round room on an upper floor contained a ballroom, used for dances with patients and members of the community.

A creaky, wooden spiral staircase leads to the indoor observation deck of the dome. On a clear day, the windows in the dome allow for views up to 30 miles. The bluffs of Illinois and the Clayton skyline can sometimes be seen from the observation deck.

In the late 1940s, the population was nearly 4,000 patients. Today, roughly 175 patients stay in the hospital building or in one of the campus apartments. The most common illness for clients today is schizophrenia or schizoaffective disorder. The average length of stay is roughly five to seven years. The facility releases about 35 to 50 rehabbed patients per year. About 75 state workers use the original building for offices. The building is very old and is in need of repair work. Some say the building is haunted and have reported hearing "conversations." The facility's librarian and archivist reported hearing voices and a book falling to the floor. The book was open to an article about the importance of a library in a mental hospital. A boulder on the front lawn marks the spot of a time capsule that was buried in 1994 on the building's 125th anniversary.

Source: Valerie Schremp Hahn / *St. Louis Post-Dispatch*, April 14, 2019

The St. Louis City Sanitarium, located at 5300 Arsenal Street, in the southwest part of the city. The older building is a five-story structure surmounted by a picturesque dome. The institution opened on April 23, 1869, and housed 125 insane persons transferred from the state asylum in Fulton. Construction of the building's west and east wings were not completed until October 1910 and January 1911, respectively. In 1948, the institution became the St. Louis State Hospital. By the 1990s, the complex was in use by the St. Louis Psychiatric Rehabilitation Center, the consolidated form of a number of institutions previously located on the site. The buildings and grounds were renovated in 1998. Photograph from the St. Louis Lantern Slides collection of the St. Louis Public Library.

St. Louis Mercantile Library at UMSL

The St. Louis Mercantile Library at UMSL is the oldest general library in continuous existence west of the Mississippi River. The library was also the first art gallery in St. Louis. Since its founding in 1846, it has remained an important cultural asset, providing members with access to several collections of books, art, and archival materials. The collections include historic newspapers and presidential and Civil War–era letters. The library plays a big part in preserving St. Louis history.

The library, known internationally for its depth and breadth of collections, currently hosts the annual St. Louis Fine Print, Rare Book & Paper Arts Fair, which connects local collectors with dealers from across the country. It remains a center for education and culture.

Source: Stephanie Wallace / *Town&Style,* April 24, 2019

The International Shoe Co.

The International Shoe Co., designed by Theodore Link, was built in downtown St. Louis in 1909. In the 1930s, playwright Tennessee Williams' father was a manager at the shoe company headquarters.

The building was also the home of a charter school until 2012. The building is now the Last Hotel, which refers to the "last," a tool used for shoemaking.

Source: Valerie Schremp Hahn / *St. Louis Post-Dispatch,* January 19, 2020

Leschen Wire Rope Company

The factory building for the former Leschen Wire Rope Company is located at 2727 Hamilton Avenue. Leschen twisted thousands of strands of wire into single lengths of steel cable to be used for cable cars, logging, mining, and suspension bridges around the world. The building is now the home of Growing Jobs Missouri, a medical marijuana company.

Source: Chris Naffziger / *St. Louis Magazine*, March 2020

Leschen & Sons, of St. Louis, exhibited its wire rope, cables, and cableway accessories in the Machinery building at the Louisiana Purchase Exposition (1904 World's Fair), March 18, 1905. Photograph from the Louisiana Purchase Exposition Glass Plate Negatives. Collection of the St. Louis Public Library.

Shanley Building

The Shanley Building at 7800 Maryland Avenue in Clayton is an architectural landmark. It is recognized as the first International Style building in the Midwest. The building, on the National Register of Historic Places, was designed by architect Harris Armstrong. After construction was completed in 1936, it won a silver medal at the Paris Exhibition of 1937 and was highlighted in both *Architectural Record* and *Architectural Review.*

Armstrong was in high demand after this project and went on to design over 100 structures in the area, including the Ethical Society of St. Louis in Ladue, the Magic Chef building in St. Louis, Cori House in Glendale, and Grant Medical Building in the Central West End. He died in 1973.

In 2019, the building was slated for demolition to make way for a new development.

Source: Joe Holleman / *St. Louis Post-Dispatch*

National City Stockyards

The railroads and stockyards are what made East St. Louis. In the early 1870s, business leaders established a stockyard on 650 acres in an area called Gallagher's Pasture. Just north of East St. Louis, the stockyard opened in 1873.

In 1907, the owners incorporated the stockyard into a town called National City. The town owned all the structures and operated its own fire and police departments. National City even owned the East St. Louis Junction Railroad, which is known as the shortest line in the U.S. at a little more than a mile long.

The National City Stockyard Bank was the depository for the large amounts of cash needed for the livestock industry. Not one bank in East St. Louis defaulted during the Great Depression because the Stockyard Bank, flush with cash, made loans to them to keep them afloat.

In the 1910s, it was common to see real cowboys on horses driving cattle down Collinsville Avenue in East St. Louis to get them to the stockyards.

At one point between World War I and World War II, the stockyard was the largest market in the U.S. for horses, mules, and hogs. It was also generally the second or third largest cattle market.

Buffalo Bill Cody would visit the stockyard when his Wild West show was in town. President Theodore Roosevelt spent the night at the National Hotel nearby. Legend has it that 1930s gangster John Dillinger passed on robbing the National City Stockyard Bank because every road out of National City risked being blocked by a train. In 1960, John F. Kennedy spoke at the stockyards while campaigning.

Business declined throughout the 1970s and 1980s. The cattle and hog auctions ended when the town was dissolved in 1997. The stockyard owners evicted everyone and made the town vanish. The area has since been annexed into Fairmont City. The last trace of the National City Stockyards, the old Armour packing plant which closed in 1959, was torn down in 2016.

Source: Joe Holleman / *St. Louis Post-Dispatch*, June 19, 2016

The Former St. John's United Methodist Church

The former St. John's United Methodist Church, designed by Theodore Link, was built in 1902. The Greek revival church was the first of three built on what was later known as "Holy Corners" at Kingshighway & Washington Boulevards. In the 1990s, the building was vacated by the church. In 2014, it was redeveloped as the Link Auction Galleries.

Source: Valerie Schremp Hahn / *St. Louis Post-Dispatch*, January 19, 2020

Lemp Brewery

Lemp Brewery, located at 3417 S. Broadway, was a victim of Prohibition 100 years ago. The massive building and the cellars beneath date from the 1860s to 1910s. Encompassing thousands of square feet, the space was used by International Shoe Co. until they pulled out in the 1980s. The building is now being used by Blue Arrow Holdings, a medical marijuana company.

Source: Chris Naffziger / *St. Louis Magazine*, March 2020

Cherokee Candy and Tobacco Company

This building at 1315 Cherokee Street was once home to the Cherokee Candy and Tobacco Company. Prior to the Civil War, this site was the location of brewer Adam Lemp's lavish Italianate country villa. The location is near the former Lemp Brewery facilities. The building is now being used by BeLeaf Medical, a medical marijuana company.

Source: Chris Naffziger / *St. Louis Magazine*, March 2020

Continental Can Company

A large warehouse, located at 7110 North Broadway, once was the site of the Continental Can Company. Located across from Bellefontaine Cemetery, this was Plant No. 73 for the company based in Connecticut. Continental Can Company switched its production over to support the war effort during World War II. The warehouse is now home to KindBio & VMO-OPS Inc., a medical marijuana company.

Source: Chris Naffziger / *St. Louis Magazine*, March 2020

St. Louis Public Library Barr Branch

William Barr of the Barr Dry Goods Co. donated land at Jefferson & Lafayette Avenues for the construction of the St. Louis Public Library. The Barr branch, built in 1906, was the first of the Andrew Carnegie–funded libraries in the St. Louis Public Library system.

In 1907, the branch hosted the library system's first story time for children. It underwent a $1.6 million renovation in 1995.

Source: Valerie Schremp Hahn / *St. Louis Post-Dispatch*, January 19, 2020

Second Presbyterian Church (third location)

The third location of the Second Presbyterian Church was designed by Theodore Link in the Richardsonian Romanesque style in 1899. President Theodore Roosevelt worshipped here while visiting the 1904 World's Fair. Gen. Dwight D. Eisenhower and Mamie Eisenhower visited the church during his 1952 presidential campaign.

The church was originally formed in 1838, and its first location was built downtown on a piece of land owned by Pierre Chouteau.

Source: Valerie Schremp Hahn / *St. Louis Post-Dispatch*, January 19, 2020

Lantern slide of 1840 drawing of the Second Presbyterian Church, erected on October 11, 1840, on the northwest corner of 5th & Walnut Streets, St. Louis, on a lot purchased from Pierre Chouteau. This structure was larger and designed by architect Lucas Bradley. 1840.

Wednesday Club Building

The Wednesday Club building was designed in 1908 by Theodore Link. The architecture included horizontal lines and a low-pitched, overhanging roof. These details were likely inspired by the Prairie styles of Frank Lloyd Wright. The Wednesday Club was a women's social organization that fought for school improvement, cleaner air, and sanitation laws. The club left the building in the 1970s and moved to Ladue.

Now the building, called the Link Auditorium, serves as a concert and event space.

Source: Valerie Schremp Hahn / *St. Louis Post-Dispatch*, January 19, 2020

Lindell Avenue Methodist Episcopal Church

The Lindell Avenue Methodist Episcopal Church was designed by Theodore Link. The church committee wanted to build a church "someplace west of Vandeventer Avenue," since many members were leaving their homes to build newer homes out west. The structure, which stood at the southwest corner of Lindell & Newstead Avenues, was built on land carved out from Peter Lindell's farm. The first service was held in 1892.

The church was eventually torn down, but the upper stones were used to build the newer Grace Methodist Episcopal Church, which held its first services in 1913.

Source: Valerie Schremp Hahn / *St. Louis Post-Dispatch*, January 19, 2020

The Academy

The Academy, now a residence in Ste. Genevieve, was the first public school west of the Mississippi. It also was the first Christian Brothers School in North America.

The Ste. Genevieve Academy, as it was known, first became a school in the early 1800s. In 1854, General Firmin

Rozier took over the property and turned it into a private boys' school. To accommodate the private school, he built an additional wing and enlarged the structure to 7,500 square feet.

The walls of the house are two feet thick. They are the original walls of Fort de Chartres. The town took stones from the French fort, which was abandoned in 1772, and hauled them up to the highest point in Ste. Genevieve County to build the structure.

In 1861, The Academy closed and was renovated to be Rozier's family mansion. The mansion remained in the family for 74 years.

Historic preservationist Timothy Conley restored the property before Frank Rolfe made it his family's home in 2005.

Source: Amanda Dahl / *Ladue News*, May 29, 2020

Random Bits

The Wainwright building, built in 1891 in downtown St. Louis and designed by architect Louis Sullivan, is known as one of the first skyscrapers in the U.S.

◁ St. Louis had the first gas station for road vehicles.

◁ Customers were known to get their own fuel behind a store at 420 South Theresa in 1905.

Sources: *St. Louis Post-Dispatch*, March 15, 2020. Jane Henderson / *St. Louis Post-Dispatch*, December 15, 2019

View from southeast of the Wainwright Building at Seventh & Chestnut Streets, St. Louis. Photograph by Lester Jones, July 31, 1940. The architectural firm Adler and Sullivan designed the Wainwright Building at 709 Chestnut Street in downtown St. Louis for St. Louis brewer and financier Ellis Wainwright. The 1891 building, now housing Missouri state offices, is on the National Register of Historic Places.

RESIDENTIAL

....

Mullanphy Emigrant Home

The Mullanphy Emigrant Home was built in 1867 at 1609 North 14th Street.

Bryan Mullanphy was the son of St. Louis's first Irish millionaire. He was also the mayor of the city in the late 1840s. When Bryan died in 1851, his will stipulated that one-third of his property be left to the city to create "a fund to furnish relief to all poor emigrants and travelers coming to St. Louis." The Mullanphy House opened to all nationalities and faiths a little more than 15 years later.

By 1877, the building closed and the Mullanphy fund began paying for the food and lodging of immigrant families elsewhere. The building was leased to the St. Louis School Board until 1899.

For most of the mid-20th century, the structure housed the factory for Absorene Manufacturing Co., which still makes cleaning sponges at their current location on Cass Avenue.

Over time, the Mullanphy House fell into disrepair. In 2006, the south wall collapsed after a storm. In 2007, the east and north walls collapsed from another storm. The Old North St. Louis Restoration Group purchased the building and began fundraising to save the building from total collapse.

The current owner is local physician Dr. Wahied Gendi. He purchased the building for $130,000 and has plans to restore it back to its original glory.

Source: Jacob Barker / *St. Louis Post-Dispatch*, May 6, 2019

Onetto Family Home

The two-story home in Elsah, Illinois, was built in the 1850s for the Onetto family. Elsah is a quaint Mississippi River hillside village. In 1931, the home was purchased by Principia College and operated as an inn for college guests for 40 years. The mini-mansion, which offers a wide view of the Mississippi River, was a Federal-style home before Italianate embellishments were added in the 1880s.

As of 2019, Kirk and Cindy Verseman own the home.

Source: Jim Winnerman / *St. Louis Post-Dispatch*, November 24, 2019

2205 Lynch Street

The home at 2205 Lynch Street in Benton Park is a Civil War–era stone home owned by Peggy Ladd since 2012. The mid-1800s structure is an example of a German peasant home. As of 2020, due to the home falling into disrepair and the high costs for rehabilitation, Peggy planned to demolish the home.

The home is located on a lot next to a historic 19th-century soda factory, which has been rehabbed by Peggy to preserve its soaring loft, wooden beams, and redbrick walls. The original structure from 1898 housed the Vogel-Buol Soda Water Company.

Source: Tony Messenger / *St. Louis Post-Dispatch*, December 8, 2019

Selma Hall

Selma Hall, also known as Selma Farm and Kennett's Castle, is a private estate on 2,400 acres in Jefferson County. It includes a 12,000-square-foot castle, 6,400-square-foot conference center, four smaller houses, hunting-and-fishing lodge overlooking a lake, shooting range, pool, tennis court, a stable, hiking and horseback trails, and an 18-hole golf course.

The castle is a nine-bedroom, six-bathroom, limestone mansion with a gun tower used in the Civil War. The structure, which includes impeccable stonework and woodwork, is modeled after the late 11th-/early 12th-century northern Italian Castello di Vezio.

The Course at Castle Ridge golf course has a 5,900-square-foot clubhouse, and its cart paths and ponds are accented by the same locally excavated limestone used to build the castle.

The conference room, which now includes meeting rooms in silos with 30-foot ceilings and a patio with a view of the pool and tennis court, was once a stable. It also includes eight bedrooms, 11 bathrooms, a kitchen, and a fitness room.

A number of influential families and companies have owned the estate. In the 1850s, Col. Ferdinand Kennett and his wife built the castle on a bluff overlooking the Mississippi River. Kennett was a dapper, wealthy gentleman adventurer from Falworth, Kentucky. The future King Edward VII of England once spent an extended stay on the estate.

For more than 30 years, Union Pacific has owned the estate and used it as a corporate retreat. In 2018, they decided to close it to reduce costs. Few outside the company have been allowed on its grounds. Union Pacific has allowed assessor personnel on the property, roughly three miles south of Festus, only a few times.

Sources: Leah Thorsen / *St. Louis Post-Dispatch*, February 12, 2020. Bryan A. Hollerbach / *Ladue News*, May 1, 2020

Vouziers Mansion

The Vouziers mansion is a French country chateau built by Joseph Desloge in 1926. The 286-acre estate is located in a wooded area near the Missouri River, just north of Florissant and just west of New Halls Ferry and Shackelford Roads. In 1996, McDonnell Douglas Corp. bought the property for $7

million to create a learning center. It is now part of the Boeing
Leadership Center.

Source: Leah Thorsen / *St. Louis Post-Dispatch*, February 12, 2020

Exterior front of Vouziers, the residence of Joseph Desloge, photographed
by Charles Trefts in 1938. Photograph from the Charles Trefts Photographs
collection of the State Historical Society of Missouri.

John Schieck House

The John Schieck House, located in Benton Park, was built in
1890. Schieck, the original owner, was a local tailor. The home
includes several great details of its original Victorian period.

Source: Amy Burger / *St. Louis Post-Dispatch*, February 9, 2020

Campbell House Museum

The Campbell House was built in 1851 on the corner of Locust
and 15th Streets for Robert Campbell. In 1822, Campbell

emigrated from Ireland to America before he joined the fur trade out West. Prior to settling in what was then St. Louis's wealthiest suburb, he befriended Native Americans and amassed a fortune. While in St. Louis, he expanded his real estate, banking, and riverboat holdings. Mark Twain actually piloted one of Campbell's riverboats.

Exterior view of the Campbell House Museum, photographed by Charles Trefts, circa 1950. Photograph from the Charles Trefts Photographs collection of the State Historical Society of Missouri.

The Gilded Age house played host to President Ulysses S. Grant for dinner. The original labor force was comprised mostly of Irish women. They would prepare up to 60 meals per day.

Eliza Rone, who worked as a nursemaid, was the only slave known to have lived at the house. In 1857, Campbell emancipated her. The emancipation could have been driven by Campbell's mother-in-law, Lucy Ann Winston Kyle, who had just moved in and, as a Quaker, despised slavery. Despite Rone's emancipation, she remained at the house as a paid worker for about 10 years. After settling in Kansas City, her husband, John, founded a Black masonic lodge and her son worked at a Black newspaper. In 1918, Rone wrote a letter to the Campbell bachelor sons, whom she had helped raise, thanking them for a Christmas gift.

Ten of Campbell's children died during childhood. Only three sons survived him, none of whom married or had children of their own. Due to the lack of an heir, an international scramble occurred to divvy up Campbell's fortune, equivalent to $69 million today.

In 1943, the house became a privately funded museum. Because of the 53 interior photographs from the 1880s discovered, the home is staged with historical accuracy and with the Campbell family's original furnishing. Some believe the house is haunted. Victoria L. Schultz, the current weekend manager, saw a motion-sensor light go on up in the cook's bedroom. She verified the house was empty with the surveillance feed on her phone.

Source: Nicholas Phillips / *St. Louis Magazine*, February 2020

The Butler House

The Butler House was built in 1892 for James Gay Butler at 4484 West Pine Boulevard in the Central West End. Butler was a prominent St. Louis tobacco manufacturer. The 6,000-square-foot house also included a carriage house. The house is currently on the National Register of Historic Places.

Source: Maggie Peters / *Ladue News*, May 29, 2020

Erastus Herrick Warner Home

The Erastus Herrick Warner home was designed in 1888 by Theodore Link. The Romanesque revival-style home sits on the edge of the Shaw neighborhood.

Warner was a lumber baron. Beautiful woodwork decorates the inside of the building, including the grand staircase that was hand-carved in Germany. Later the home served as a funeral home, a bank, and a livery. It now is used by Mental Health America of Eastern Missouri.

Link designed a similar home next door for writer J. W. Buel, but it was razed in the 1920s for the Saum Apartments.

Source: Valerie Schremp Hahn / *St. Louis Post-Dispatch*, January 19, 2020

BUSINESSES AND BRANDS

Most people know St. Louis as a beer town. But not many realize that at one point, St. Louis was also the largest producer of shoes and tobacco in the country. We have a unique mix of businesses that are based in St. Louis, from large companies like TUMS to smaller businesses like Old Vienna, the producer of Red Hot Riplets. My mother once hosted a St. Louis-themed party, which featured several different stations of food, snacks, and drinks made in St. Louis. This included well-known brands such as Ronnoco Coffee and Kaldi's Coffee and lesser-known brands like Switzer's licorice and Dad's Cookie Company.

When I visit my aunt in Chicago or sister in Minneapolis, I always bring with me a St. Louis goody bag. This generally includes an assortment of St. Louis snacks and sauces, including Billy Goat Chips, Country Bob's all-purpose sauce, Thomas coffee, Hendrickson's salad dressing, and Urban Chestnut beer.

While some of the following businesses and brands are well-known and some are obscure, all of them played a part in the history of the area.

Dierbergs

In 2020, the family-owned grocer Dierbergs Markets celebrated its 166-year anniversary. In 1854, the first country store in Creve Coeur opened on Olive Street Road. Greg Dierberg is the current president and CEO. Greg's sister, Laura Dierberg Padousis, is the current vice president and secretary. Laura and Greg are the fourth generation of Dierbergs to manage the business. It now has 24 stores in the St. Louis metro area and one in the Lake of the Ozarks.

Sources: Carol Enright / *Out & About*, April – June, 2020; Jen Roberts / *DesignSTL*, July – August, 2020

Schnucks

Schnucks was founded in 1939 by Anna Donovan Schnuck, grandmother to the current owners. The original location was in North St. Louis. Anna's husband, Edwin, was in the wholesale meat business. Their children (Ed, Annette, Don) each opened up their own store. The pork steak was invented by Don and Ed. In 1947, the family began reorganizing their seven stores. In 1952, they incorporated the business as Schnucks Markets Inc. Most of the company's growth has come by way of acquisitions. In 1970, Schnucks acquired the Bettendorf Rapp chain. In 1995, they acquired National. In 2018, they acquired Shop 'n Save.

Source: Jen Roberts / *DesignSTL*, July – August, 2020

Straub's Fine Grocers

In 1901, William A. Straub opened his first store in Webster Groves. Every day, William would visit residents to collect orders, fill the orders back at the store, and deliver them later in the day by horse and buggy. Trip Straub is the current president and CEO. Straub's has been offering high-quality specialty foods and fresh meals prepared in store for four generations.

Source: Jen Roberts / *DesignSTL*, July – August, 2020

St. Louis Car Co.

St. Louis Car was founded in 1887 at 8000 Hall Street in North St. Louis. In the 1890s, business grew exponentially, and St. Louis Car bought out two competitors: Union Car Co. and Laclede Car Co. The company focused primarily on building buses and trolleys during World War II. It also made gliders, seaplanes, and amphibious landing vehicles for the war effort.

St. Louis Car Co. was one of the 10 largest employers in the area in the 1950s. After being bought by General Steel Industries in 1960, it focused mainly on building subway cars for transportation systems in New York and Pennsylvania. The cars were known for their silver, stainless steel exterior and bench seating on the inside. In 1969, New York City transit officials bought roughly 400 of the 44-seat R-42 cars. They were the first cars on the NYC line to be completely air-conditioned. Most of the cars were retired between 2006 and 2009. In 2020, the last R-42 subway cars built by the old St. Louis Car Co. had their final run in New York. Two R-42 cars have already been memorialized. The two cars used in the subway chase scene in 1971's Oscar-winning *The French Connection* can be seen at the New York Transit Museum.

The company also built the trams that carry people to the top of the Gateway Arch. In 1967 on the first day the trams operated, the company president, Edwin B. Meissner Jr., was one of the first riders to the top. St. Louis Car Co. ceased operations in 1973.

Source: Joe Holleman / *St. Louis Post-Dispatch*, February 11, 2020

Ladue Market

Ladue Market was a grocery shop that opened in 1928 at the corner of Clayton & South Price Roads. They sold meat, produce, and specialty items. It was a place where workers knew customers by name, and customers could charge items to their house account. Staffed by five generations of the same family, the business simply couldn't compete with the grocery chains any longer. Jerry Meyer, who worked behind the counter for 50 years, said, "We're not on the same buying tier as some of the big stores, and that definitely puts us at a big disadvantage." After 91 years in business, the store closed its doors in 2020.

Source: Rachel Rice / *St. Louis Post-Dispatch*, January 6, 2020

Irene's Mayonnaise

Charles Bolin was a city mover and shaker. He owned American Thermometer Co., was in the insurance business, was president of the St. Louis and St. Charles Bridge Co., ran Grand Avenue Bank, and owned the St. Louis Crystal Water and Soda Co. He was also an investor who helped bring Kellogg's Corn Flakes to the market.

In 1905, Charles was working in the insurance industry when he visited the Battle Creek Sanitarium in Michigan to be treated for gout. After trying the corn flakes there, he thought they could be marketed and convinced Will Kellogg to start his own company. Charles lent Kellogg $30,000. Kellogg spent most of the money on advertising, so he was unable to repay Charles. Charles took Kellogg to court, but the Supreme Court of Michigan said the company was too new and the stock value was young.

Charles had five children. In 1922, he gave his son Ray a house on Aberdeen Place in Clayton and the St. Louis Crystal

Water and Soda Co. as wedding presents. Ray's son, Charles R., became vice president of the company. The plant was located where the Ronnoco Coffee Co. sits today.

Irene, the wife of Charles R., loved to cook. Charles R. left the family when their son Charlie was nine years old. Irene gave Charlie her cookbook before she died in 1995. He noticed her recipe for homemade mayonnaise was not included, so he asked her to write it down. She gave him the recipe, along with a note that said, "Good luck, son." Charlie was a butcher with Schnucks and Straubs for roughly 10 years. He found himself without a job in 2008 and thought of his mother's mayonnaise. The next year, Charlie put Irene's Fresh Homemade Mayonnaise on the St. Louis market.

Source: Valerie Schremp Hahn / *St. Louis Post-Dispatch*, June 24, 2018

Schenberg's Market

Schenberg's Market was the first grocery store chain in St. Louis. Mitchell and Rose Schenberg married at age 16 when living in the old Jewish neighborhood on the north side of downtown. They opened the first store a year later in 1914 at Broadway Avenue & Keokuk Street in South St. Louis. Despite being a produce man at heart, he diversified his offerings by carrying other grocery items. By 1931, the couple had opened four more stores (at South Grand Avenue & Chippewa Street, Meramec Street & Virginia Avenue, Kingshighway & Devonshire Avenue, and Cherokee Street & Ohio Avenue) as well as at least one produce wagon downtown, which was managed by Mitchell's father.

The family built a large home on Telegraph Road in Lemay, at a time when that area was mostly farms and woods. The house was built of white stone and had a large veranda. It sat on 14 acres with a pool, tennis court, and a small dance hall. In the late 1930s, the chain's manager embezzled money, causing the family fortune to decline. The family had to sell off four of the five stores, with the South Grand store the only location remaining.

View of the building that housed Schenberg's Market at the southwest corner of California and Gravois. A sign for James Printery can be seen next door. Photographed by Richard W. Lemen, circa 1930.

In the 1940s, Mitchell and Rose opened four new stores: 39th Street & Lafayette Avenue, 12th Street & Park Avenue, the Delmar Loop, and Clayton Road & DeMun Avenue. Joe Schenberg, one of the founder's four sons, was responsible for the produce purchases and ran the family's wholesale produce warehouse at 806 North Third Street during this growth period. They also opened a store at Gravois & Mackenzie roads in Affton in the 1960s. In 1965, Joe left the family business and sold life insurance for 50 years before retiring in 2015. Lasting more than 50 years, the last Schenberg's Market, located in the Delmar Loop, closed in

1969. Rose died at the age of 53 in 1951. Mitchell died at the age of 81 in 1978.

Source: Joe Holleman / *St. Louis Post-Dispatch*, August 27, 2017

TUMS

In 1928, the formula for TUMS was developed by St. Louis pharmacist Jim Howe, whose wife had indigestion. The pure, sweet, fine tablets are simply made of calcium carbonate (also known as limestone or chalk). Ancient Sumerians actually had their own recipe of milk, peppermint, and sodium carbonate. But the calcium carbonate lasts longer. Jim's wife handed out the homemade meds to seasick passengers on a cruise, causing their popularity to grow.

Jim then started the Lewis-Howe Co. with his uncle, and they set up a radio contest to name the product. In 1930, the name "TUMS" came from a nurse at Jefferson Barracks.

In 1978, Lewis-Howe Co. was sold to Revlon. In 1985, Revlon split up, selling off the subsidiary that oversaw TUMS. In 1986, the Beecham Group bought that subsidiary. In 1989, the Beecham Group merged with SmithKline. In 2000, SmithKline merged to form GlaxoSmithKline, the owner as of 2020.

TUMS have been made in St. Louis for over 90 years. The business is located in a five-story redbrick building by Busch Stadium. TUMS sells more than 60 million bottles or rolls per year, which is double the total of the second-place Rolaids. The tablets are now offered in a variety of flavors, some sugared and some sugar-free.

When Menlo Smith heard from mothers that his Pixy Stix product was too messy, he ran the powder through the presses at the next-door TUMS factory and created the SweeTARTS.

Source: *St. Louis Magazine*, December 2018

Cook's Imperial Champagne

Cook's Imperial Champagne was made by the American Wine Co., located inside a castle-like stone building in North St. Louis. The vast network of underground cellars was below where Vashon High School is now located at Cass & Garrison Avenues. They meandered through an area about a block square roughly 50 feet underground, with a spring flowing into one of them.

Isaac Cook, a Chicago politician, started the company in 1859 and named it after himself. The champagne was made mostly with California grapes. At one point, it was the number one–selling champagne in the country. A 1916 newspaper advertisement read, "We may live without friends; we may live without books, but civilized man cannot live without Cook's Imperial Champagne." Playing to the medical community during Prohibition, one ad in a medical journal read, "In atonic dyspepsia, vomiting, and in convalescence from acute diseases, Cook's Imperial Champagne is held in high esteem by physicians."

During Prohibition, the supply likely came from a makeshift plant in an old inn near what is now Highway 141. Officials found 453 quart bottles of the finished product, 215 gallons in copper vats, and 800 gallons of "mash" in a barn. They arrested seven men and one woman and destroyed all of the alcohol. A 1925 story in the *Post-Dispatch* read, "Paul K. Gill, a prohibition agent, recently detected the odor of mash struggling for supremacy over gasoline fumes as his roadster chugged past Caruso's Inn on Clayton Road, two miles west of Altheim."

After Prohibition, the business took off again. Strangely, the company had a brush with Nazi Germany. Hitler's foreign minister, Joachim von Ribbentopp, married into the family that owned the winery. Joachim sold the products in Europe, but he never invested in the St. Louis business.

Sales in September 1941 at the American Wine Co. were up 95 percent, thanks to the halting of importation of French wines during World War II. At that time, there were 100 workers at the plant, double the number of workers before the war. In the 1950s, the business closed, and the building was turned over to a vinegar company.

The building was demolished in the 1970s. When the new Vashon High School was being built in 1999, the site was excavated and a stone stairwell that went down into the lower vaults was discovered.

Cook's Champagne is now produced by Mission Bell Winery in Madera, California.

Source: Valerie Schremp Hahn / *St. Louis Post-Dispatch*, December 30, 2018

Levison & Blythe

Levison & Blythe, an ink company, was started in 1854. It operated several locations in downtown St. Louis before closing its last store at 612 North Second Street in the 1950s. In 1877, a newspaper reported on the company's elaborate display booth at a fair on what is now Fairground Park. Its signature colors (violet, scarlet, black ink) flowed through "a glass fountain of fanciful form."

In 1896, their building on the 200 block of North Third Street, where the Gateway Arch grounds are today, was located next to a building that caught on fire. That fire set off 300 pounds of gunpowder stored in another building, causing an explosion heard from Union Station. Six people were killed and several dozen were injured, most of them Levison & Blythe employees.

Source: Valerie Schremp Hahn / *St. Louis Post-Dispatch*, February 25, 2018

S. G. Adams

S. G. Adams, an ink company, was started in the 1870s. Free orchid corsages for the first 100 ladies and free punch and St. Louis bicentennial auto stickers for everyone were touted in a 1964 advertisement for a three-day store opening in Crestwood Plaza. It was known during its later years as a stationery store specializing in selling maps. According to the *Post-Dispatch* in 1991, in order to follow the war in the Persian Gulf, people were buying maps from the store. It closed its last retail store downtown in 1994.

Source: Valerie Schremp Hahn / *St. Louis Post-Dispatch*, February 25, 2018

Buxton and Skinner

Buxton and Skinner, an ink company, started in the 1870s around the time mass production of typewriters began. An 1892 newspaper ad mentioned the manager of the caligraph department, W. H. Williamson. A caligraph is an early typewriter.

The company printed a well-known map of the 1904 World's Fair. It also produced ink, marketing a special brand called "Cote Brilliante," which means "bright hill" or "shining hill" in French. (An American Indian mound, where Kingshighway and Martin Luther King Drive now meet, went by the same name.)

The building was located at Fourth & Olive Streets. Buxton and Skinner sold various office supplies, including ashtrays and sheet-metal desks that offered "proof against fire, vermin, mice, and dampness" according to a 1913 ad. The business was sold to Mail-Well, another printing company, in 1999.

Source: Valerie Schremp Hahn / *St. Louis Post-Dispatch*, February 25, 2018

View of the gardens surrounding Pumping Station No. 1 at the Bissell's Point waterworks in St. Louis, printed by the Missouri Post Card Co. and Buxton and Skinner Litho in St. Louis, circa 1900.

Schaeffer Manufacturing

Schaeffer Manufacturing was started by Nicholas Schaeffer in 1839. Nicholas arrived in America as a teenager in 1830. His first stop was Baltimore. When leaving Baltimore, his horses were stolen so he walked and took a flatboat to Cincinnati. While in Cincinnati, Nicholas apprenticed in a soap and candle factory. Later when settled in St. Louis, he started two soap factories: one under where the Arch is today and another at the western edge of downtown.

Nicholas's best friend, Eberhard Anheuser, owned a soap and candle company. Eberhard's company burned in the 1849 fire, but one of Nicholas's factories survived. The two businesses then merged, becoming Schaeffer Anheuser Soap and Candle Manufacturing Co. The area where Schaeffer's factory was originally located is now in between the two legs of the Gateway Arch.

At the beginning, Schaeffer Manufacturing Co. made soaps, candles, and natural oils. Black Beauty Grease, one of their products, lubricated the wheels of covered wagons heading west. The grease was also used by miners in Alaska to prevent frostbite on their faces, and to fry their eggs. The grease was made from animal fats, so it was safe to eat (despite the fact that the eggs turned black). Another product called Red Engine Oil was used to lubricate steamboats. Referencing the 1849 Gold Rush and the wagon wheels that needed grease, an old ad read, "We lit the way in '49."

The partners eventually purchased a struggling brewery, Bavarian Brewery, and Eberhard wanted to invest more money in it. Nicholas asked that Eberhard buy him out. At that time, Nicholas reportedly said, "There's a brewery on every street corner. Soap's where it's at." Eberhard invested in the brewery and got Adolphus Busch, his son-in-law, to join him in the venture. This is the birth of Anheuser-Busch.

Nicholas was an early St. Louis millionaire, but the panic of 1870 caused him to lose most of his personal fortune. The company survived, and Jacob Schaeffer, Nicholas's son, took over the business in 1880 when Nicholas died. Sales of the slab soap that Schaeffer sold out of barrels declined when a floating soap, Ivory, was developed by Cincinnati candlemaker William Procter and soapmaker James Gamble. Schaeffer's candle business dissipated after Thomas Edison found a way to create light without candles and the 1904 World's Fair displayed electric lights. Schaeffer pivoted to focus on oil and grease products.

In 1917, Jacob's son-in-law, William Shields, took over the company. In 1947, William's sons, Gwynne and Tom Shields, took over. Around this time, Schaeffer was manufacturing the grease and oil that lubricated postwar machinery. Gwynne and Tom died suddenly in the early 1980s, so John Shields left his job with IBM to take over the family business with his sister Jackie. They put 50 percent of the family-owned stock in an irrevocable trust for the next 100 years, meaning the company can't be sold.

The company is now located between the Arch and Anheuser-Busch, at 102 Barton Street. Schaeffer Manufacturing Co. now makes synthetic motor oils, hydraulic fluids, and diesel fuel additives. John Schaeffer Shields was the company's board chairman until he died in 2016 at age 90. John's son, Jay Schaeffer Shields, has served as the president since 2006 and represents the fifth generation of the company. The company reached its sales goal of $150 million in 2017, with goals for future growth. It is widely known as the oldest company in St. Louis.

Source: Valerie Schremp Hahn / *St. Louis Post-Dispatch*, April 29, 2018

Absorene Manufacturing Co. Inc.

Absorene Manufacturing Co. Inc. was founded by H. R. Henderson in 1891. The company manufactures dough that is used to clean wallpaper, paintings, paper, and other surfaces. In 1927, Henderson moved the business to a brick building built in 1867 at 1609 North 14th Street, which was previously the Mullanphy Emigrant Home. The now vacant building still has the "H. R. H." initials on the front in white tile.

Absorene may be the last wallpaper cleaner maker remaining. Sales peaked in the early 1940s, when coal dust filled the air and the now-white Old Courthouse was black with pollution. When city leaders made changes to tackle the problem, homes switched to oil and gas heat, and housewives didn't need to clean wallpaper anymore.

For several years, they sold children's play dough, marketed with the names Romper Room, Howdy Doody, and Walt Disney. Absorene's competitor, Play-Doh, made a modeling compound in the 1930s that before becoming a popular children's item was also marketed as a wallpaper cleaner. But Absorene made it first. At one point, the company also produced Red Devil Roach Destroyer, which was a combination of arsenic and flour.

Ralph Coldewe Jr. bought the company in 1976. Steve Coldewe, Ralph's son, is the current president. They are the third owners of the business.

With the same recipe, the Coldewes start up their 1940s-era mixer a few times a year to make batches of the "pink blob" to sell to restoration companies, museums, and janitorial suppliers. In 1996, the company moved to a warehouse at 2141 Cass Avenue, near the National Geospatial-Intelligence Agency (NGA) campus. Their factory is located in the St. Louis Place neighborhood. The red container read, "A dry cleaner that works like an eraser. Absorbs dust and dirt out of ANY KIND of paper while it cleans." Old ads called it a "ball of magic." The Absorene mascot was known as the "Wallpaper Wizard."

The focus of their business now is making and distributing various sponges. This includes horse and tack sponges, cosmetic sponges, and pet hair removal sponges. The dental industry has used Absorene to make bridge molds. Fishermen have used it as bait. A funeral home director used it as filler for crash victims because Absorene absorbs moisture better than what funeral homes usually used. The Missouri Historical Society conservators use the company's soot sponge in their work.

Source: Valerie Schremp Hahn / *St. Louis Post-Dispatch*, January 28, 2018

Blanke-Wenneker Candy Co.

Blanke and Brothers Candy Co. started in 1849. The company merged with the Wenneker Candy Co. in 1904.

A household name in St. Louis, Blanke-Wenneker was known for producing chocolate "direct from the bean" and buttery Nadja Caramels. Ads ran for "girls wanted" to pack Sweetheart popcorn, pack and dip chocolates, and wrap stick candy and caramels. In 1914, the company ran an advertorial in the *St. Louis Star-Times*. A front-page article detailed the arrival of entertainer Bonnie Burr and promoted her theater appearance that night. The article highlighted Blanke-Wenneker's chocolates and claimed she visited the factory in disguise. "All chocolates are hand-dipped by young women experts, using the most expensive coverings... Finished candies are whisked away into the packing room and kept covered until they are put into a beautiful box, ready for you. There is not chance in the world for a speck of dust to get on them," the article read.

The factory, which employed hundreds of people, was located on Market Street where Kiener Plaza now stands. The company president, Charles F. Wenneker, was a generous man who was active in social circles. His name was mentioned as a possible Republican candidate for mayor. Early in his career, his three young daughters died of scarlet fever within three days of one another. Late in his career, he left the company after breaking his leg while getting out of a car at a Clayton restaurant. In 1915, Wenneker left town without telling his wife, Johanna, where he was going. While on a train in Salt Lake City, Charles told a reporter that he lost over $50,000 in cash and investments in steel stocks and was "practically penniless." In the late 1920s, the company went out of business.

Wenneker eventually returned to St. Louis to be close to his aging mother. He worked menial jobs and managed a lodging house in St. Louis before breaking his arm and retiring. Wenneker died at age 83 in 1936. One biography mentioned he had one living daughter. His obituary listed only his wife and two brothers as survivors. Wenneker is buried near his daughters in a family plot at St. John's Cemetery in Bellefontaine Neighbors.

Source: Valerie Schremp Hahn / *St. Louis Post-Dispatch, March 25, 2018*

Random Bits

♩ When Prohibition was lifted in 1933, Anheuser-Busch sent a case of beer to President Franklin D. Roosevelt.

Source: Harry Levins / *St. Louis Post-Dispatch*, June 12, 2020

GEOGRAPHY, PARKS, STREETS, MONUMENTS, LANDMARKS, SCHOOLS

Where do I begin? This is where I get to do the most exploring, researching down a rabbit hole. Next time you go to a park, take a look at the name of the park. If it is named after a person, there is likely a good amount of history involved. Who was that person? Was the parkland originally part of that person's estate? Is that person's house still on the property? Look closely, it may be. Keep an eye out for a monument or marker; it may contain some information on the person who donated the land for the park. One of my favorite parks in St. Louis is Tilles Park in Ladue. Not only is it a wonderful park that I visit frequently with my family, but it is one of those parks with which most St. Louisians are familiar but don't ever think about who "Tilles" was. Not many people know that Andrew "Cap" Tilles acquired his fortune from cigar, real estate, stock, and brokerage businesses. At one point, he was the largest owner of horse racing tracks in the country, making him one of the most politically powerful people in the history of U.S. horse racing.

One marker I am still stumped by is located in Kirkwood Park. Near the pond, there is a stone marker with the name

"Mary Sanders Benton" on it. After some online searches, I have not been able to find anything. But I am still working on it.

Photograph of the Mary Sanders Benton marker at Kirkwood Park. Photograph taken by the author, 2021.

Streets? My goodness. This is where you can really spend some time. There is generally a good amount of history behind most street names. A newer subdivision in Chesterfield? Probably named after the farm on which the houses were developed. Near my house in Kirkwood, I noticed several street names are associated with golf (Bogey Lane, Par Lane, Fairway Lane, etc.). At one point in time, there was a golf course located where Woodlawn Avenue now runs. Bodley Avenue in Kirkwood? Harry Innes Bodley was one of the founding fathers of Kirkwood. I could go on and on.

I hope the following facts encourage you to look curiously at different statues, street signs, and park names the next time you are out and about.

Friedrich Jahn Memorial

Friedrich Jahn was considered the father of gymnastics. In 1811, he founded a gymnastic and social society, the Turnverein. He believed physical fitness led to moral superiority. A memorial for Jahn sits just east of Art Hill.

Source: Valerie Schremp Hahn / *St. Louis Post-Dispatch*, July 3 – 9, 2020

Semicircular seating area in Forest Park, with a large bust of Friedrich Ludwig Jahn, the founder of modern gymnastics, at the midpoint, flanked by statues of youth preparing to throw a shot put and a javelin. Photographed by Charles Trefts. Photograph from the Charles Trefts Photographs collection of the State Historical Society of Missouri.

Poertner Park

Poertner Park is comprised of 27 acres at 4064 Hencken Road in Wildwood. The land was donated to the city by Joanna Yost, a longtime Rockwood School District teacher and resident of Wildwood. The property was known as the William Poertner Farmstead. It has seven structures, including six barns and storage buildings built between 1920 and 1930, and a single-family, ranch-style home built in 2001. The land includes a mix of pasture and woodlands and a one-acre pond.

The site is maintained as an undeveloped wildlife refuge and preserve for picnicking, bird watching, hiking, and fishing.
Source: *St. Louis Post-Dispatch*, June 9, 2020

Lindenwood Water Tower

The redbrick water tower on the Lindenwood University campus stood for over 120 years. As part of the city's history, it was treasured by St. Charles residents as an icon. Lindenwood University was founded by Mary Easton Sibley as a school for women in 1827. To expand the school, Sibley and her husband George Sibley bought 500 acres of land. Construction started on Sibley Hall in 1856, and it was expanded in 1886.

This image is part of the S1083 John J. Buse, Jr. Collection, which consists of photographs, scrapbooks, historical notes, correspondence, and personal reminiscences of a St. Charles historian and collector between 1860 and 1930. Photographs by St. Charles photographers Rudolph Goebel, John Gossler, and A. Ruth are included. 1881.

The first water tower was built by St. Charles on the site in 1887. In 1896, it was destroyed by a tornado. In 1898, St.

Charles built the iconic tower we know of today. It remained in use until 1955. A wrought-iron railing at the top of the tower held a neon sign that read "Lindenwood College" from the 1920s through the 1950s. The tower was originally on city-owned property adjacent to the campus. In 1971, the school, once known as the "Wellesley of the West," bought the tower from the city for $1.

In 1980, the tower was officially designated as a St. Charles historic landmark. It was fully restored in 1997. But after falling into disrepair over the years and being deemed structurally unsafe, the tower was scheduled for demolition in 2020. The school said it will save 100 of the tower's bricks and sell them to the public.

Sources: Joe Holleman / *St. Louis Post-Dispatch*, May 15, 2020; James Kintz / *St. Louis Post-Dispatch*, May 13, 2020

Bloody Island

Bloody Island was originally a sandbar that first peeked from the Mississippi in 1798. Over time, it grew and threatened to cut St. Louis off from riverboat traffic. For 50 years, high-society men used the island to settle their disputes by dueling. If you were a wealthy member of society at that time, you owned a pair of dueling pistols. If you felt that your reputation had been challenged, you settled it with a duel.

In 1817, Senator Thomas Hart Benton was shot in the knee by Charles Lucas. When he returned for another round, he killed Lucas.

In 1823, Thomas C. Rector killed Joshua Barton in their duel.

Benjamin Gratz Brown, the editor of the *St. Louis Globe-Democrat*, was shot in the leg by Thomas Reynolds on Bloody

Island in 1856, which resulted in a permanent limp. They were dueling over emancipation.

The land mass is now part of the Illinois shore. If you look across the river toward the eastern pylon of the Eads Bridge, you are looking at the southern tip of Bloody Island.

Source: *St. Louis Magazine*, April 2018

Water Works, 1842, illustrated from the view of Bloody Island and published by the St. Louis Water Division.

Howell Island

Before the Daniel Boone Bridge was built in 1937, the only way for Chesterfield residents to cross the Missouri River was by ferry. Residents traveled from the end of Olive Street Road at Eatherton Road to Weldon Springs in St. Charles County by way of Lewis' Ferry. John Lewis owned 420 acres in the area now known as Faust Park. In 1810, Lewis sold the land to Frederick Bates, who was elected the second governor of

Missouri in 1824. Bates would ride his horse to Lewis' Ferry, stable the horse near the landing, and ride the ferry across the river where he kept another horse. From there he rode to St. Charles, the state capitol from 1821 – 1826.

In 1853, James Howell bought the Lewis' Ferry and land holdings in Bonhomme Bottoms. Howell also owned a large tract of land in St. Charles County. After acquiring Lewis's land, Howell established a settlement known as Howell's Landing. Later, this area became known as Centaur. Some early residents of Howell's Landing included William Tyler, Martin Boisselier, and Thomas Bayer. Bayer owned a blacksmith shop, and all three men were farmers.

An island of 3,000 acres on the south side of the Missouri River channel is known as Howell Island. In 1804, when Lewis and Clark first recorded the island, it was only 400 acres and was located on the north side of the channel. In 1900, Anton Leiweke bought the island and cleared it for farming. After acquiring the ferry business, he carried farmhands and supplies to the island on barges pushed by a small vessel known as the "Honeybell." Wild turkeys and other wildlife were abundant on the island until the flood of 1903. The deer population grew until the flood of 1951. Domestic cattle were known to swim the channel to Howell Island and form herds of wild bovines. From 1905 until 1931, the wild bovines were hunted on the island as dangerous animals. The last 75 were rounded up in 1931.

In 1945, a German Navy POW boat camp docked at Centaur. Over four months, the prisoners built a causeway to Howell Island and repaired the levee. In 1953, Harold Hill bought Howell Island for $80,000. In 1978, the Missouri Department of Conservation acquired the island. In 1993, the entire island was under water in the Great Flood of 1993.

Today, despite the causeway being frequently under water, the island offers biking and hiking trails in addition to limited hunting and fishing. On November 2, 2015, a family of three went to the island to enjoy the outdoors. They became disoriented and could not find their way off the island. Water and air support were used to rescue the family.

Source: Ann Chrissos / *Out & About*, July – September 2018

St. Louis Caves

St. Louis has nearly 50 caves, more than any other city. Many of the caves were used to help make beer. Lemp Brewery used the caves to ferment its lagers. Bootleggers used them to hide their alcohol. The caves, many of which are below Interstate 55 and are between 65 to 85 feet below the city streets, feature streams, waterfalls, old uranium deposits, unique cave formations, and burial grounds of prehistoric animals.

After an archaeological dig was conducted on a lot at 3314 Lemp Avenue, items were found that were consistent with traditional African religious rituals. A cowrie shell, once used as currency in parts of Africa, was also found at the site. It is likely that African Americans lived in the small one-room cottages in that area after the Civil War. One of the cottages at 3318 Lemp is still standing. The cottages were built for people, mostly African Americans and German immigrants, who worked at Lemp, Falstaff, and Anheuser-Busch breweries.

The caves actually attracted German brewers to build in the area since they helped keep their beer cooler during summer months. As many as 40 breweries were atop the limestone caves in south and central St. Louis by 1860. There were once five breweries clustered where the Anheuser-Busch brewery is today.

Located below the southwest corner of Jefferson & Washington Avenues is Uhrig's Cave. The cave was named for German immigrants and brewers Franz and Ignatz Uhrig. In 1852, the Uhrigs bought the property and the limestone cave below. They extended the 40-foot-long cave to 210 feet and added brick walls and arched ceilings. They also added an underground narrow-gauge railroad that ran from the cave to Uhrig's Brewery at 18th & Market Streets. The Uhrigs put $100,000 into developing the cave, which is equivalent to roughly $2.7 million today. By the 1870s, they had turned it into the top nightlife spot in the city. By 1900, the popularity of the cave waned, and a roller rink and bowling alley concept failed. In 1908, developers built an exhibition hall called The Coliseum that hosted several presidential primaries and nationally known entertainers. In 1953, the cave was closed and razed for construction of Jefferson Bank and Trust Co.

Moonshine Cave was a distillery 40 feet underground at the corner of Franklin & Jefferson Avenues. U.S. agents eventually discovered it.

In 1945, a businessman named Lee Hess bought the Cherokee Cave and the DeMenil mansion. While living in the mansion, Hess fixed it up and began to turn the cave into a tourist attraction.

While digging out the clay blocking some of the cave's passages to make it more accessible, workmen discovered large deposits of animal bones. Researchers from around the country traveled here to see the bones from armadillos, peccaries, and an extinct subspecies of a woodchuck thought to be 20,000 years old. The woodchuck subspecies was named *Marmota monax hessi* after Lee Hess.

In 1950, Cherokee Cave opened as a tourist cave and museum with an entrance near South Broadway & Cherokee Street, at 3400 South Broadway. For $1, visitors could explore a mile-long cave system and see the bones, old brewery lagering rooms, murals depicting the history of St. Louis, mannequins dressed in Roman costumes, a "dry" zoo, and the Damascus Palace. The palace, more than 1,000 years old, was brought to America from Damascus in 1893. It was shown at the St. Louis World's Fair in 1904. Also, tourists could see streams, waterfalls, cave formations, and a burial ground for prehistoric animals.

Cherokee Cave is a combination of Minnehaha Cave and Lemp Cave, which before commercial refrigeration was used as brewery storage in the 1860s. The major breweries, Falstaff, Lemp, and Anheuser-Busch, opened up shop here because of the caves.

In 1961, the Missouri Highway Department bought the property to build Interstate 55, razing the museum and sealing off the entrance in the process. The DeMenil mansion, which currently operates as a house museum, was saved by The Landmarks Association of St. Louis and Union Electric. Roughly 75 percent of the cave still exists. There is still one locked entrance on private property. The Damascus Palace was purchased by a local television executive. The St. Louis Science Center has a few of the skull and bone fragments from a peccary, and during renovations to their newly acquired building in 2016, Earthbound Beer discovered a beer cave carved from the same limestone as Cherokee Cave. Earthbound excavated this cave and now uses it for storage and special events.

Sources: *St. Louis Magazine*, December 10, 2016; Joe Holleman / *St. Louis Post-Dispatch, February 14, 2019*; Valerie Schremp Hahn / *St. Louis Post-Dispatch*, April 23, 2017

Wirth Property

In 1886, the Wirth property was at the center of Altheim, Missouri, a small farming community. The Altheim Inn and Fette Tavern served as gathering places for farmers. One of the closest buildings to the north was the Oge Log Cabin, which served as the post office and has since been reconstructed at Drace Park.

In 1890, the Wirths built their blacksmith shop on the property. Until the 1930s, the blacksmith shop served as a gathering place for the community.

St. Louis has a rich history of gathering places, frequently known as Groves. In the early 1900s, there were several Groves along many of the east and west roads in St. Louis. The closest building to the east was Busch's Grove, located on Price Road. Chesterfield Grove was located next to what is now Annie Gunn's. Schaeffer's Grove was located across the street from what is now Chesterfield Elementary School. Tower Grove eventually became a city park. These Groves were gathering places for farmers to host community dances, town meetings, and parties on Saturday nights.

The Wirth property is now the site of the Town & Country Town Square.

Source: Skip Mange / *Town & Country Newsletter*, Spring 2017, Vol. 33, No. 1

Ferry Roads

Dougherty Ferry does not cross a body of water, but it does come within two miles of the Meramec River, south of Big Bend Avenue in Valley Park. In 1833, Thomas Dougherty received a license to operate a ferry. On his first license, the river was spelled "Maramec," the same spelling used for the state park near St. James. On other licenses, the river was spelled as "Merrimack." In 1843, a license to operate a ferry was issued to Alfred Dougherty. Other than Alfred Dougherty being a resident of St. Louis proper according to a census, little is known about the Dougherty family. It is not known if Thomas and Alfred were related.

Lemay Ferry crosses the Meramec River into Jefferson County and becomes Jeffco Boulevard in Arnold. In 1833, Louis Trudeau was granted a license for a ferry in that area. It was known as Catalan's Ford. In 1834, a Francois Lemay was granted a ferry license. Lemay was a terrible ferry operator, and in 1848, thanks to the St. Louis County courts, Noah H. Whitmore took over the license. While the river cross was known as Lemay Ferry, the road was called Carondelet Road, Middle Road, or Meramec Road until the 1850s. After improvements were made to the road, it became known as Lemay Rock Road or Lemay Road. Starting in the early 1900s, the road was referred to as Lemay Ferry.

Tesson Ferry crossed the Meramec River into Jefferson County, becoming Highway 21. In 1837, John B. Tesson received a ferry license. One member of the Tesson family, Jean-Baptiste Tesson, died in the 1840s. Jean-Baptiste had a daughter who married into the very prominent Sappington family. John B. Tesson could be the English-style spelling of Jean-Baptiste Tesson.

Hall's Ferry got its name from an operation on the Missouri River between St. Louis and St. Charles counties. In 1805, Sarah James ran a ferry in that area. Her family is the namesake of Old Jamestown. In 1813, Phinehas James bought the land from his mother, Sarah, and leased the ferry operation to

Edward Hall. In 1816, Phinehas sold the land to Rufus Easton, the founder of Alton and a well-known lawyer and politician. Hall continued to operate the ferry, and when the road was surveyed, it became known as Halls Ferry Road, or Road No. 1. Today, Halls Ferry Road runs from near Shackelford Road in Old Jamestown to the Baden area of St. Louis.

In 1848, the land and ferry were purchased by Reuben and Lydia Musick. The ferry's name changed to **Musick's Ferry**. Today, just across the Missouri River from New Halls Ferry Road in St. Charles County is a Music Ferry Road. The Musicks were very successful. In addition to the booming ferry business, they also operated a store, tavern, grist mill, quarry, sawmill, and Musick's Inn. The inn, built in 1850, was a 19-room stone building that provided ferry customers with accommodations. Musick's Inn operated into the 1910s and was demolished in the late 1930s.

Morgan Ford Road

Morgan Ford Road got its name from the man who ran the shallow crossing of River des Peres, although Morgan's first name is unknown. It runs from Arsenal Street at Tower Grove Park to south St. Louis County where it becomes Union Road, crossing over River des Peres along the way.

William Russell bought a parcel of land bounded by Arsenal Street, Gustine Avenue, Chippewa Street, and Kingshighway. He called the area Oak Hill. William eventually sold the land to his brother, James Russell. The stretch of Morgan Ford Road that ran from Arsenal to near Chippewa was once known as Russell Lane. One of James Russell's grandsons was Charles Marion Russell. Charles, born in 1864 in Oak Hill, was a well-known cowboy artist who moved to Montana in the 1880s.

Source: Joe Holleman / *St. Louis Post-Dispatch*, January 24, 2016; January 31, 2016

Chippewa & Morganford, photographed by Richard W. Lemen, June 10, 1931.

Fyler & Morganford, photographed by Richard W. Lemen, February 8, 1932.

Castle Wall in Fairground Park

A castle wall that can be seen in the southeast corner of Fairground Park, near Grand and Natural Bridge, is the only structure left from St. Louis's first zoo. Made with brick, stone, and four crenellated turrets, it once housed bears. In 1856, the land that is now Fairground Park was the site of a large annual Agricultural and Mechanical Fair. The fairgrounds included a three-story palace for displaying poultry, a half-mile horse racing track with a grandstand, and an amphitheater that could hold tens of thousands of spectators.

During the Civil War, the amphitheater was converted into a hospital by the Union Army. The fairgrounds combined with adjacent land became the Benton Barracks.

Drawings of buildings in St. Louis's first zoological garden, which was constructed in 1876 on the grounds of the Agricultural and Mechanical Association Fairgrounds. The original zoo garden included a bear pit, aviary, monkey house, and carnivora house. This was the forerunner of today's Saint Louis Zoo in Forest Park.

After the war, the fair organizers decided to assemble a zoo. In 1876, several structures, including the fortress wall, were built. It was deep enough to hold the bear pits, which became the main attraction. Over the years, the zoo added llamas, antelopes, tapirs, kangaroos, and a water hog. Children could enter the zoo for 10 cents, while adult admission was 25 cents.

At times, the zoo was chaotic. One groundskeeper was gored by a buffalo and witnessed his clothes ripped by a leopard. An old lioness refused to enter her crate and had to be subdued with ropes. A black wolf escaped, causing a five-mile chase. A panther screamed after being lured into a box with a piece of meat and locked inside.

Due to financial difficulty, the animals were publicly auctioned in 1891. The animals were bought by the Ringling Brothers, private citizens, and the city of St. Louis. With plans for a new zoo in Forest Park, the city bought a herd of elk, a zebu cow, and a bull camel named Clint. The city bought the fairgrounds land in 1909 and renamed the area Fairground Park. The bear pits now serve as storage space for the parks department.

Source: *St. Louis Magazine*, June 2020

Union Station Tower Clock

The clock in the tower of St. Louis Union Station is one of the oldest, most notable clocks in St. Louis. It has been running for over 126 years. In 1894, architect Theodore Link designed the building and modeled it after the ancient wall around the city of Carcassonne in southern France. According to some, Link's draftsman Harvey Ellis designed the 230-foot clock tower.

Until the Gateway Arch was completed in 1965, the clock tower was the first impression of St. Louis for many. In 1978, the last passenger train left Union Station.

Inside the clock tower is a 30,000-gallon water tank that was stored there in case of fire. The tank is held up on a four-legged metal frame. In the 1940s, the station stopped using the tank. The tower was also used to ventilate air throughout the station. A smaller tower that runs up the corner of the large tower includes vents that took in air that ran over hot radiators inside. That air was used to warm up the train offices and station. Wooden stairs with 30-inch banisters lead up the tower, which is closed to the public.

Designed by architect Theodore Link, Union Station opened in St. Louis in 1894. At the time of its opening, it was the busiest and largest railroad station in the world. On the opposite side: "Published by The St. Louis News Company, St. Louis – 1900."

St. Louis Clock and Gear Work, Fred Phillip and Son made the clocks. All four clock faces, which originally cost $850, are made of opaque white glass and measure about eight feet in diameter. An old mechanism in the tower controlled all four faces of the clock for several years, but it was eventually replaced with electronic clockworks.

The clock that greets guests in the Grand Hall lobby area of the St. Louis Aquarium is modeled after the old tower clock. It is part of a more than 10,500-gallon tank filled with colorful discus fish and rummy-nose tetras. PGAV Destinations designed the clock, which is nine feet in diameter with laser-cut aluminum numbers.

Source: Valerie Schremp Hahn / *St. Louis Post-Dispatch*, March 1, 2020

Westland Acres

Westland Acres is a historically African American community located between the municipalities of Chesterfield and Wildwood. It is tucked off of Church Road in the northeast area of Wildwood. Some refer to the area as "The Hill" due to its high position atop a tall, tree-covered hill.

The area was founded by William West, a free man who was one of the area's first settlers. Previously enslaved by the Long family, West accumulated enough wealth to buy roughly 133 acres of land from Long in 1867. West paid about $6 per acre. When West died, the property was divided among his seven children. The land has since been divided even more among additional generations, including the Frazier family.

The Frazier family currently owns roughly 90 acres. Clifford Frazier was one of West's great-grandsons. Clifford was married to Doris, who owns much of the Westland Acres land today. When Doris moved to Westland Acres, they did not have gas, water, bus service, or mail service, and all the kids went to one school.

At the community's center is Union Baptist Church, which has served as a meeting place for the community since before 1921. The church burned in 1977, but Clifford helped to rebuild it in 1984.

The community has dwindled from about 50 families to nine remaining households. For years, due to rising raw land tax rates, the community has been on the state's Places in Peril list compiled each year by The Missouri Alliance for Historic Preservation.

Source: Jessica Meszaros / *West Newsmagazine*, January 9, 2019

Chesterfield and Bellefontaine Schools

Chesterfield School, built in 1908, was a one-room schoolhouse in the Chesterfield area. Residents of eastern Gumbo and the town of Chesterfield attended Chesterfield School. Chesterfield School was located at 16758 Wild Horse Creek Road. The first school board members were Robert Coulter, president; Frank Glaser, clerk; and Albert Wilmas, director. In 1924, the original wooden school building burned down. In 1925, a larger brick structure was built on the same site.

In 1951, a new Chesterfield School, part of the Rockwood School District, was built at 17700 Wild Horse Creek Road, four miles west of the original school. The first principal of the new school was Garlin Kellison, a teacher from Bonhomme School. In 1960, the old brick school was purchased by Frank Bube, who converted it into his private residence. The brick structure has since been demolished.

Chesterfield School also had a second building, located on Wild Horse Creek Road, for African American students. The students were descendants of slaves who were brought to the area by the early settlers, such as the Longs, Caulks, and Bacons.

Residents of Bellefontaine, also called Hilltown, attended Bellefontaine School. It was located at 14950 Conway Road. In 1860, Samuel Conway and his wife Mary Ellen sold over 31 acres of land along Conway Road for one dollar to Maury Eberwein, George Smith, and Joseph Brookes, who were trustees of School District Number Four. Samuel Conway was the son of Joseph Conway Sr., a pioneer in the area. A one-room schoolhouse was built on one acre of land, and by 1896, the student population had increased enough that a two-room brick schoolhouse was needed.

In 1911, the school board members were George Burkhardt, president; Herman Stemme, clerk; and H. M. Seiler, director. The school offered the "three Rs" — reading, 'riting, and 'rithmatic — plus rhythm band performances, plays with historical themes, and formal graduation ceremonies. The school became part of District 27 in 1910.

In 1954, the school became part of the Parkway School District. In 1960, Parkway sold the building to Norman J. Sutter, who converted it into his private residence. The August Hill gated community sits on the site today.

Several of the last names of students who attended the original Chesterfield School and Bellefontaine School are still seen throughout Chesterfield today: Hilltown Village Center, August Hill and Lydia Hill Drives, Eberwein Dog Park, Stemme Drive, Herman Stemme Office Park, Burkhardt Place, Eatherton Road, Swingley Ridge Road, Schoettler Road, and Fresh Air-Weinrich Heating and Cooling Company.

Source: Ann Chrissos / *Out & About*, January – March 2019

Lake School

Lake, MO, was a village located along Olive Street Road and Hog Hollow Road. One of the residents, Nannie T. Stevens, donated a plot of land for a school. In 1897, a 25- by 60-foot one-room schoolhouse was built across the street from the Quathem property. The inside included rows of double desks, a blackboard, a potbellied stove, a cloak room, bookshelves, and a teacher's desk. The structure was built with white wood and included black shutters, six windows, and a bell cupola.

In the early 1920s, Lavern Reising was the teacher. The building became obsolete as the student population increased to 62 by 1925, so E. W. Zierenburg bought the original school building and moved it diagonally across the street to be behind his Mercantile Store. The structure was used as a storage shed until it was purchased by Louis Gilber in 1967. Gilber donated the building to the Creve Coeur-Chesterfield Historical Society. At a cost of roughly $1,600, it was then moved to a park on Coeur de Ville Drive in Creve Coeur. It is now a museum to showcase what schools and life were like at the turn of the 20th century.

In 1925, a bigger brick school was built on the original site after the Lake School was moved the first time. The school operated until 1948, when it became part of the Fern Ridge District. The structure was then sold and used as a private residence.

Around 1900, Frank Storch donated an acre of land for a second Lake School that would educate African American children. This school was located west of River Valley Drive. Roughly 13 children attended the school. Most of the students were from the Brooks and James families, descendants of slaves who had lived in Hog Hollow (Lake) during the Civil War. The school was eventually demolished.

The area also had a one-room church school, The Old Stone Bonhomme Church. It was built in 1841 and located on Conway Road. The ground level housed a one-room school and a small living area for the teacher, who was generally always a male.

Source: Ann Chrissos / *Out & About*, April – June 2019

St. Charles Street
St. Charles Street in downtown St. Louis was originally known as Vine Street. Between 10th and 14th Streets, it now serves as an alley for clubs and restaurants on the south side of Washington Avenue. The street ends at Jefferson Avenue.

The original portion of the street, from Leonor K. Sullivan Boulevard to Fourth Street, has been removed for the Gateway Arch grounds, an interstate highway, and apartment towers. Pierre Chouteau and Antoine Soulard owned fur warehouses on this portion of the street.

St. Louis's first billiard table was in a public house at Vine & Second Street. In 1780, Mr. Vige bought the billiard table for about $110, to be paid in fur pelts over three years.

A blockhouse was built in 1789 at Vine & Third Street to protect settlers from attacks, after an attack by Sauk and Fox Indians. In 1816, the Mansion House Hotel was built at Vine & Third Street. It served as the first seat of government for the Missouri Territory. In 1820, the hotel hosted the meetings that led to the creation of the Missouri Constitution.

In 1840, the building, then known as City Hotel, was bought by Theron Barnum. Theron was a cousin to P. T. Barnum, the legendary carnival king. In 1849, under Barnum's ownership, the hotel was the site of a notorious murder. Wealthy French brothers with aristocratic lineage, Gonsalve and Raymond de Montesquieu, checked into the hotel. Later that night, Gonsalve was on the hotel patio and fired several shots through a window, killing one man and wounding another. When guests came outside to see what was going on, Gonsalve killed another man and wounded two more. Diplomacy played a big part in the trial as both French and U.S. officials encouraged local judges to issue a lenient ruling. Gonsalve was convicted before being pardoned by Missouri Governor Austin A. King. After the brothers returned to France, Gonsalve died in an insane asylum.

Other buildings that fronted on St. Charles Street were the United Hebrew Congregation, on the southwest corner of Sixth Street & St. Charles, and St. Luke's Hospital, on the southeast corner of 10th Street & St. Charles.

In 1888, the hotel was demolished. Today, Gentry's Landing apartments sit on this site.

Source: Joe Holleman / *St. Louis Post-Dispatch*, March 13, 2016

View of Walgreens pharmacy on left and several people on the busy street. Photograph by Richard W. Lemen, November 9, 1931.

Firefighters' Monument at Bellefontaine Cemetery

A 15-foot marble monument, erected in the early 1870s, stands on lot No. 1922 in the northeast quadrant of Bellefontaine Cemetery. The plot around the monument is the burial site of John W. Bame, the fourth chief engineer of the St. Louis fire department, from 1867 to 1869. In the early years of the fire department, the fire chief was known as the "chief engineer." The first three St. Louis chief engineers are also buried elsewhere at Bellefontaine.

The plot, roughly 95 feet by 100 feet, is owned by the St. Louis Firemen's Fund Association. In addition to maintaining the plot, this society pays small benefits to disabled and retired firefighters. In 1869, the fund bought the plot for $1,772.

Around 1915, the helmet on the monument disappeared. In an effort to replace the helmet, former firefighter and local sculptor Robert Daus created a solid brass helmet weighing 50 pounds.

Source: Joe Holleman / *St. Louis Post-Dispatch*, October 1, 2016

Chesterfield's 'Stonehenge'

Chesterfield has an ancient celestial calendar that stretched 3.56 miles across the entire Missouri River valley. It included a sacred cave, two earthen pyramids, a temple, and mortuary building. A 1,000-year-old lost city was discovered perfectly sealed under six feet of flood-deposited soil in the Chesterfield Valley.

The Dampier site, as it is known, was a massive civic, market, and ceremonial complex with strong ties to the powerful pyramided capital city that stretched from St. Louis to the Cahokia Mounds State Historic Site. Among several other buildings discovered at the site were a large L-shaped temple, which overlooked the Chesterfield Valley, and a mortuary building.

The largest surviving earthen pyramid in St. Louis County, Blake Mound, is also located along the Chesterfield bluffs, adjacent to the Dampier site. It was built directly above a cave, which is located at the base of a limestone bluff. The mound is constructed with eight million pounds of hand-dug and hauled material. This alignment of the mound and the cave just below it served as a physical representation of those people's world view: the pyramid reaching upward into the heavens, a mortuary complex in the world of the living, and the cave serving as an entrance into the underworld.

When seen from the L-shaped temple's entrance, the sun seems to rise directly out of Blake Mound during the winter solstice dawn and out from behind the mortuary building across the village at dawn of the summer solstice.

Source: Mark Leach / *Out & About, October – December 2017*

Old Powder Depot Gate

A gate at Jefferson Barracks Park that leads to an overlook was made of four U.S. Army cannons. The fence was made of deactivated Civil War rifle barrels from the St. Louis Arsenal south of downtown. The gate led to the powder depot headquarters. Bayonets can still be seen on top of some of the barrels. The oldest item in the park, a Jefferson Barracks display stone from 1827, can be seen in the Powder Magazine Museum.

Source: Valerie Schremp Hahn / *St. Louis Post-Dispatch*, May 5, 2019

Stone Powder Magazine at Jefferson Barracks, circa 1933. Photograph from the Historic American Buildings Survey collection of the Library of Congress Prints and Photographs Division.

Sylvan Springs

Sylvan Springs is the actual spring where Commander Stephen Watts Kearny camped with his troops in 1826, two days after a deed was signed to establish an infantry school at Jefferson Barracks. More than 100 years later, public workers built a beer garden at the site. A natural amphitheater nearby held World War II troops that watched Judy Garland, Bob Hope, Danny Kaye, and Joe Lewis perform. The spring is now part of Sylvan Springs Park, separate from Jefferson Barracks Park.

Source: Valerie Schremp Hahn / *St. Louis Post-Dispatch, May 5, 2019*

No. 1 Garage

No. 1 garage, near some gas pumps just off CCC Road in Jefferson Barracks, , was built originally as a powder magazine. It is now used for storage. The vault was built to fall down and extinguish a fire in the event of an attack or accident. You can see a stone etching with the date "AD 1866" above a doorway. A manhole on the floor leads to a cave. Within the cave, a large archway is blocked by stone. Legend has it that the blocked archway is the entrance to a tunnel that leads to the site of the ordnance commander's house, which no longer exists.

Source: Valerie Schremp Hahn / *St. Louis Post-Dispatch*, May 5, 2019

Stone Foundations and 'Pneumonia Gulch'

Throughout Jefferson Barracks, about 20 concrete foundations are visible. The foundations were used to support wooden structures built for World War II officers. The foundations down by the river were intake centers, where soldiers received their uniforms and medical checks after they got off the train. The foundations in the woods closer to the Lemay Pavilion were offices and living quarters for higher-ranking officials. The soldiers stayed in tents atop a wooden platform, called a hutment. Soldiers frequently got sick with respiratory infections due to sinkholes in the area that collected water. Because of this, the nickname for the area was "Pneumonia Gulch." To this day, a rusty axle from a military vehicle can be seen coming up from the ground near one swampy spot.

Source: Valerie Schremp Hahn / *St. Louis Post-Dispatch*, May 5, 2019

Quarry and William Clark Campsite

Just behind the amphitheater at Jefferson Barracks Park is a limestone cliff where workers quarried stones to build the powder magazine and stone walls. Workers would drill to insert a wooden peg and either ice or heat it to expand the peg to split open the rock. William Clark passed by the quarry, which faces the Mississippi river, in 1803 on his way to Cahokia to meet Meriwether Lewis.

Source: Valerie Schremp Hahn / *St. Louis Post-Dispatch*, May 5, 2019

Laborer's House Gardens and Fruit Cellar

The Laborer's House is next to the visitor's center at Jefferson Barracks Park. In the gardens behind the house, you will see stone foundations for walls and a privy that once supported a summer kitchen for the Laborer's House. In a patch of woods behind the Laborer's House is an underground fruit cellar, likely used by those who lived in the house.

Source: Valerie Schremp Hahn / *St. Louis Post-Dispatch*, May 5, 2019

Jefferson Barracks Laborer's House, circa 1933. Photograph from the Historic American Buildings Survey collection of the Library of Congress Prints and Photographs Division.

North Gate with Alligator Insignia

Two guard shacks and a building at the north entrance of Jefferson Barracks Park were used by military police during World War II. You will see the Coat of Arms of the 6th Infantry above the doors of the buildings. The insignia features a green alligator, representing the service of the regiment during the Seminole War of 1837. The green ladder underneath the alligator represents the storming of the Citadel of Chapultepec in Mexico in 1847. During World War II, German owners of nearby bars in Lemay received permission to employ some of the German POWs, of which there were nearly 500 housed at the barracks. Seven German and Italian POWs who died at Jefferson Barracks are buried at the cemetery there.

Source: Valerie Schremp Hahn / *St. Louis Post-Dispatch*, May 5, 2019

Spanish Naval Gun, Sundial, and Swastika

In 1898 during the Spanish-American War, the armored cruiser *Oquendo* of the Spanish Navy was sunk near Cuba. One of the salvaged guns was placed just behind Building One at Jefferson Barracks Park overlooking the Mississippi River. Next to this rare gun is an iron fence surrounding a replica sundial. The original sundial was stolen decades ago. It is thought the sundial was used to help keep time for the trains that brought troops to the station. Just below the sundial sits a swastika and the name "Belke" carved into the top of a stone wall. It was possibly carved by a German POW.

Source: Valerie Schremp Hahn / *St. Louis Post-Dispatch*, May 5, 2019

Building No. 1

Building No. 1 is a three-story administration building built in 1900. The building, not normally open to the public, contains a second-floor ballroom. On a back wall of the ballroom is a large topographic map of Jefferson Barracks which details locations of buildings long gone and the sinkholes in the area of Pneumonia Gulch. The map was painted by Private Ralph V. Rausch in 1938.

Source: Valerie Schremp Hahn / *St. Louis Post-Dispatch*, May 5, 2019

Building No. 1 was part of the early 1920s effort to build modern hospitals for U.S. military veterans. The building continued to serve as an administrative facility at the St. Louis VA Medical Center, Jefferson Barracks Division from the 1920s through the 1990s. It is now used as an educational facility by the hospital. Photograph by James Stewart, circa 1933.

Nurses' Quarters and Streetcar Station

The nurses' quarters building was built in the late 1930s. It is located next to the Telephone Museum. The building is now used by St. Louis County Parks for storage of archives, including military saddles, and as a sign shop. Jefferson Barracks was the birthplace of the cavalry division, the United States Regiment of Dragoons. Six nurses shared three beds in small dorm rooms, using the beds in shifts. A gray brick building behind the nurses' quarters was once a station for a streetcar line that went along Gregg Road into St. Louis.

Source: Valerie Schremp Hahn / *St. Louis Post-Dispatch*, May 5, 2019

The nurses' quarters were built in 1939 as part of a New Deal-era improvement campaign at the U.S. Veterans Hospital at Jefferson Barracks. The building continued to serve as nurses' quarters through WWII and the postwar era, then was converted to administrative use for the St. Louis VA Medical Center, Jefferson Barracks Division in 1980. Photograph circa 1933. Photograph from the Historic American Buildings Survey collection of the Library of Congress Prints and Photographs Division.

Harvest Time in Chesterfield

Until 1988, Chesterfield was an agrarian society. Cash crops and kitchen gardens for family use were abundant in the area. Harvesting began in July and ended in October. Chesterfield's fertile soil helped to produce large crop yields.

In July, peaches were picked and sold at roadside stands, and neighbors helped each other to thresh their wheat. As technology improved, one of the more successful farmers would buy a threshing machine, which he would lend to his neighbors. While previously the men, women, and teens helped work the fields, the thresher allowed the women to spend their time preparing and serving food while the men gathered the wheat. Typically, meals were served at breakfast, midday, dinner, midafternoon, and supper.

In August, potatoes and melons were harvested. In September, corn and apples were harvested. Pumpkins were harvested in October.

Originally, horse- or mule-pulled wagons hauled the cash crops to downtown St. Louis so they could be sold and transported on Mississippi River barges. Later the crops traveled downtown by trucks.

In 1914, the Fred Schuttenberg farm was located on the present-day site of the Doubletree Hotel, near the headquarters for Reinsurance Group of America.

In 1933, the Fred Schiller farm was located on the north side of Wild Horse Creek Road and west of Long Road.

Lydia and August Hill sold peaches from their orchard at a stand located on Clarkson Road near present-day Chesterfield Mall.

In the 1940s, the Albert Fick farm was located on Wild Horse Creek Road on the present-day site of the Miramonte Subdivision.

Walter H. Stemme had a potato field in the Gumbo area. The Kummer farm and Hellwig farm were adjacent to his property.

Around 1910, the Al Wilmas farm was located in the bottoms along the north side of Chesterfield Airport Road across from Andy Kroeger's store, which is now the present-day Smoke House.

Around 1949, John and Clarence Prestien had a roadside fruit stand in front of their home at 13342 Olive Street Road.

Source: Ann Chrissos / *Out & About*, July – September 2020

Frontenac Estates

Louis de Baude, also known as Comte de Frontenac, was

the governor of New France in the 17th century. He founded Fort Frontenac, a fur-trading post in Quebec City supporting explorations west and fighting off the Iroquois and the British. He died in 1668.

In 1893, the land where Frontenac now stands was mainly hunting grounds and farmland. In the 1930s, St. Louisans Benjamin and Lora Woods stayed at the 600-room luxury hotel Chateau Frontenac in Quebec City. They were so impressed with the hotel that when they bought land off of Spoede Road in St. Louis County, they named the subdivision Frontenac Estates. This was one of the town's first subdivisions. In 1948, the village of Frontenac was officially formed.

Source: Valerie Schremp Hahn / *St. Louis Post-Dispatch*, March 17, 2019

Random Bits

◁ From 1930 until 1943, about 460 buildings on 37 city blocks were destroyed to make way for the Jefferson National Expansion Memorial. This area is now called the Gateway Arch National Park.

◁ It once took a 40-minute carriage ride to get from downtown to Forest Park.

Sources: Jane Henderson / *St. Louis Post-Dispatch*, December 15, 2019;

Valerie Schremp Hahn / *St. Louis Post-Dispatch*, July 3 – 9, 2020

St. Louis Gateway Arch (originally Jefferson National Expansion Memorial) under construction. Constructed by Eero Saarinen from 1947 – 1965; dedicated 1968. Photograph by Balthazar Korab.

The Old Cathedral in St. Louis during construction of the Gateway Arch. Construction of the Arch was completed on October 28, 1965. Photograph from a lantern slide presentation for the 1964 bicentennial of St. Louis's founding in 1764. Circa 1964.

OBJECTS

This might take a little more effort on your part, but if you look around, there are plenty of opportunities to catch a glimpse of unique historical St. Louis objects. Two of my favorite spots to search and find these are the National Museum of Transportation in Kirkwood and the Missouri History Museum in Forest Park. The National Museum of Transportation features an incredible collection of trains, automobiles, trolleys, and cars. Several of them, including a Missouri River towboat and a 1901 St. Louis Motor Carriage Company car, have special ties to the area. While this isn't an object, I encourage you to look with a curious eye at the southwest corner of the property, where you will see one of the Barretts Tunnels, a pair of railroad tunnels that were the first to operate west of the Mississippi River.

One of my most memorable moments at the Missouri History Museum was attending the "Coffee: The World in Your Cup and St. Louis in Your Cup" exhibit with my mom and stepdad. Not many people understand how big a part coffee played in St. Louis's history. In 1920, the St. Louis Chamber of Commerce labeled St. Louis as the coffee capital of the country. It was so fun to see old and new labels, cans, bags, logos, and other memorabilia from companies like Old

Judge Coffee, Ronnoco, Safari Coffee, and C. F. Blanke Tea and Coffee Company.

There are plenty more objects to find at places like the Saint Louis Zoo, Faust Park, Forest Park, and Grant's Farm.

Wurlitzer Organ

Jim Quashnock owns a Wurlitzer organ that has connections to an amusement park that operated along South Broadway Avenue near River des Peres for roughly 70 years. The area, now home to a roller rink, bus stop, and shuttered building, is bordered by South Broadway, River Des Peres, Water Street, and Catalan Avenue.

In 1928, the organ was made by Wurlitzer in Tonawanda, New York. It was then sold to the Allan Herschell Co., which sold organs with the carousels they manufactured. The 640-pound organ was sold to a St. Louisan named Sauter in 1930.

In 1896, Mannion's Amusement Park opened. In 1925, Alois Sauter, the park manager, acquired the business. The park was then renamed Sauter's Amusement Park. Sauter was a German immigrant who worked in the saloon and grocery business in the Lemay area until 1898. That year, he bought the Continental Hotel & Saloon on Lemay Ferry Road.

In the 1920s, Sauter died and the hotel and amusement park were inherited by his son, Gus Sauter. Between 1929 and 1930, Gus invested heavily in the park. He bought new rides, including a roller coaster known as The Flash, and a Herschell Co. carousel.

In 1941, the park declared bankruptcy due to lingering economic effects from the Great Depression. A group of trustees then bought the park. In 1943, it was known as The Downs amusement park. In 1953, the park closed, and the items were put up for auction (the organ was not included in the list of auction items). It operated as a public pool for roughly 15 more years.

Source: Joe Holleman / *St. Louis Post-Dispatch*, January 29, 2017

The St. Louis Carousel

Forest Park Highland on Oakland Avenue announced in 1929 the installation of its new attraction, the $30,000 St. Louis Carousel. The carousel was built in 1921 by the Dentzel Company of Philadelphia, Pennsylvania. It has 60 hand-carved horses, four deer, and two sleighs.

In 1963, the amusement park was destroyed by fire, but the carousel escaped major damage. St. Louisan Howard C. Ohlendorf purchased the Carousel in order to keep it in the St. Louis area. In 1965, he donated the Carousel to the St. Louis County Department of Parks and Recreation and supervised its installation at Sylvan Springs County Park. The St. Louis Carousel operated at Sylvan Springs until 1979, when it was obvious that the elements were taking their toll. The St. Louis County Historic Buildings Commission started to study ways to restore the Carousel and place it in a climate-controlled facility to ensure its preservation.

In 1987, the Carousel was opened in its present building at Faust Park. The Faust Park Foundation was formed to raise funds for the Carousel's continual maintenance and restoration. It is still operational at Faust Park to this day.

Source: Faust Park Foundation

Marie Thérèse Cerré's Wedding Clothes

Seventeen-year-old Marie Thérèse Cerré married 35-year-old Auguste Chouteau in 1786. The marriage resulted in nine children. In their wedding-clothes portrait, Marie's dress was donned by Beatrice Chouteau Turner. Auguste's coat was donned by another Auguste Chouteau.

In 1929, two years after Beatrice herself wed, people flocked to the old Jefferson Memorial to see department store mannequins wearing the Chouteaus' wedding clothes. A newspaper writer wrote: "First to meet the visitor's eye — and one judges it would be the first, even in a dark cellar at midnight — is the gorgeous wedding coat of Auguste Chouteau, pale green with rose lapels and lining, over a vest of Joseph-colors, including red and yellow." Today, the dress is carefully stored in a wide, flat drawer in a climate-controlled warehouse. The light pink with mint piping dress was appropriately fancy for a girl with a $3,000 dowry and a trunk full of gauzy dainties and hand-embroidered table linens.

Source: Stefene Russe / *St. Louis Magazine, January 2020*

1904 World's Fair Souvenir Plate

Darlene Rich is in possession of a white ceramic plate that shows a picture of Ulysses S. Grant's son, Fred, on horseback in front of Hardscrabble, the cabin in south St. Louis County Grant built for his young family in 1856. Grant's wife, Julia, did not like the cabin. She said it was "so crude and homely I did not like it at all. I got out all my pretty covers, baskets, books, etc., and tried to make it look home-like and comfortable, but this was hard to do. The little house looked so unattractive that we facetiously decided to call it Hardscrabble."

After three months at the cabin, the family moved to Julia Dent Grant's nearby family farm, known as White Haven. The cabin and the land it was on changed ownership a few times, and at one point, it was owned by businessman William Vanderbilt in order to help Grant cover a loan.

In 1891, real estate businessman Edward Joy had the log structure disassembled and relocated to Old Orchard in Webster Groves. The street where the cabin sat is still called Log Cabin Lane.

Frederick Dent Grant (center), son of President Ulysses S. Grant; Cyrus F. Blanke (left), president of C. F. Blanke Tea & Coffee Company of St. Louis; and a military officer pose on horseback in front of the log cabin built by Grant's father in the mid-19th century when he farmed in St. Louis County, a few days before the cabin was moved to the Louisiana Purchase Exposition grounds. Exhibited at the 1904 World's Fair, it was later purchased by August A. Busch and moved to "Grant's Farm," the Busch estate on Gravois Road in St. Louis County. Blanke owned the cabin at the time of the exposition. Byrnes Photographic Co., 1903.

In 1903, Joy sold the cabin to C. F. Blanke Tea and Coffee Co. for $8,000. The company rebuilt the cabin on the grounds of the 1904 World's Fair. For 10 cents, adults could tour the cabin. During the tour, they could buy lunch, drink coffee and tea, and buy souvenirs, including plates like the one Darlene owns now. So many souvenirs were made and left over after the fair that they ran an ad in the newspaper a couple of weeks later to promote Grant Cabin cups, vases, spoons, and other items left over from the fair.

The owner of the coffee and tea business, Cyrus Blanke, was so successful that he was the first person in the city to have a whole trainload of coffee delivered to his plant. In 1920, the St. Louis Chamber of Commerce boasted that St. Louis was the coffee capital of the nation. In 1935, after some financial difficulties, the company's assets were ordered sold. The business managed to continue until the death of Cyrus Blanke in 1942.

The C. F. Blanke Tea and Coffee Co. building now houses offices and luxury condos at South 14th & Papin streets. "C. F. Blanke Building" is carved above its entrance.

Blanke wanted the cabin to remain in Forest Park after the fair, but he and city leaders could not come to an agreement on maintenance of the cabin. In 1907, he sold the cabin to August Busch Sr., who relocated it to the beer baron's estate on what is now called Grant's Farm. For decades, the cabin was not maintained and eventually fell into disrepair.

In 1978, it was restored and reopened to the public with a big ceremony. The cabin on Grant's Farm is not far from the original location, which is now known as St. Paul's Churchyard. A plaque at St. Paul's Churchyard marks where the cabin once stood.

Source: Valerie Schremp Hahn / *St. Louis Post-Dispatch*, May 21, 2017

Random Bits

- A plaque at the Old Courthouse notes it as the place where slaves Dred and Harriet Scott filed suit for their freedom in 1846.
- A plaque at the Old Courthouse notes it as the place where Joseph Pulitzer bought the *St. Louis Dispatch* at a public auction in 1878.

Bust portrait print of Dred Scott, facing slightly left, dated June 1887. Illustration by the Century Company from the Biographical File Filing Series of the Library of Congress Prints and Photographs Division.

St. Louis Court House, St. Louis. Exterior view. Circa 1903. Photograph from the Library of Congress Prints and Photographs Division.

- An engraved marker at Kiener Plaza notes it as the start of the first trail heading west; the Boone's Lick Trail was also known as St. Charles Rock Road (which became the country's first interstate highway).
- A plaque halfway down the steps at the base of the Gateway Arch marks where the Mississippi River rose to its highest level ever at 49.58 feet in 1993. In 2019, the river crested at 46.02 feet, the second-highest crest in history.
- A gasoline-powered carriage was built in St. Louis in 1898.

Sources: Valerie Schremp Hahn / *St. Louis Post-Dispatch*, April 3 – 9, 2020; Jane Henderson / *St. Louis Post-Dispatch*, December 15, 2019

PEOPLE

This is probably the topic I read about the most. The towns of O'Fallon (Missouri and Illinois) are both named after John O'Fallon, at one point one of the wealthiest people in the country and related to explorer William Clark. It is said that at one point, he sat on the boards of half the businesses in St. Louis.

It is fun for me to not only research prominent, well-known families like the Busch family, but to take it a step further and see who the descendants are. What are their last names? What are they doing now? After you do some digging, you will recognize a lot of relations and connections. For example, several of the original founding families (Cerré family, Papin family, Gratiot family) of St. Louis are branches of the Chouteau family.

Any time a new donation is made to a cultural destination in St. Louis, such as the new Nature Playscape area in Forest Park or the Saint Louis Zoo, chances are that donor was a successful, prominent person with history of record behind their last name.

Here are some of the people who were instrumental in political affairs, civic affairs, business, philanthropy, and shaping our area as we know it today.

Wayman Smith III / 1940 – 2020

Wayman Smith III was known for being very influential in St. Louis political and civic affairs. He graduated from Soldan High School and received a bachelor's degree in business management from Monmouth College in New Jersey. After law school at Howard University, Smith became the director of conciliation for the Missouri Human Rights Commission. He also practiced law with Margaret Bush Wilson, a national and local NAACP leader.

Following in his father's footsteps, he was elected to his first four-year term as alderman of the 26th Ward in 1975. Known for his temperament and patience, Smith helped start the aldermanic Black caucus in the 1970s. After serving three terms, he was appointed by then Gov. Mel Carnahan to serve on the city's Board of Police Commissioners from 1996 until 2000. For a period of time, he was the police board president.

As a vice president at Anheuser-Busch, Smith was integral in securing the financial support for the United Negro College Fund and several other charitable and minority organizations.

At different points in his career, he was a St. Louis municipal judge and a city Airport Commission member. Smith sat on the boards for the National Sickle Cell Association, the St. Louis Symphony Orchestra, the Missouri Athletic Club, the national Urban League, the Urban League of Metropolitan St. Louis, and the Congressional Black Caucus Foundation. He also chaired the governing panels at Harris-Stowe State University and Howard University.

At the time of his death, Smith was living in Creve Coeur.

Source: Mark Schlinkmann / *St. Louis Post-Dispatch*, September 15, 2020

Virginia Minor / 1824 – 1894

In 1867, Virginia Minor helped to establish the Women's Suffrage Association of Missouri. She served as the organization's first president. In 1872, Minor attempted to register to vote for an upcoming election. Because she was a woman, the registrar in St. Louis refused to let her. Arguing that the Constitution granted women citizenship, which also included the right to vote, Minor and her husband filed a civil suit, which eventually made it to the Supreme Court. While the U.S. Supreme Court ruled against her, she continued to be an advocate for women's suffrage around the world.

Virginia Louisa Minor, head-and-shoulders portrait, facing right. Photograph by J. A. Scholten; engraving by J. C. Buttre after photoprint by J. A. Scholten, circa 1850 – 1893.

The defeat in the legal system prompted suffragists to focus on legislative change. In 1889, she testified before the U.S. Senate. In 1916, St. Louis hosted the Democratic National Convention. As male delegates walked to the convention being held at the former St. Louis Coliseum, women lined

Locust Street wearing white with yellow sashes and held yellow parasols in a silent but powerful protest. After decades of fighting, America ratified the 19th Amendment in 1920, which said citizens could not be denied the right to vote on the basis of gender.

Minor is buried in Bellefontaine Cemetery in St. Louis, which is where the county executive who denied Minor the right to vote also happens to be buried.

Sources: Diana Lambdin Meyer / *AAA Midwest Traveler*, July / August 2020; Aisha Sultan / *St. Louis Post-Dispatch*

Anthony F. Sansone Sr. / 1927 – 2020

For decades, Anthony F. Sansone Sr. was a fixture of the St. Louis region's business and political elite. As the founder of Clayton-based commercial real estate firm Sansone Group, he built some of the region's busiest shopping centers and was often close with local leaders. Sansone was the son of Italian immigrants and attended night school at Washington University to earn his real estate license. He founded his real estate firm in 1957, and over the decades, the firm grew to over 350 employees, managing roughly 10 million square feet of property.

As a young man, he ran the successful 1965 campaign for former St. Louis Mayor Alfonso Cervantes that unseated Mayor Raymond Tucker. After his win, Cervantes appointed Sansone's brother and real estate partner, Joseph C. Sansone, as city assessor.

Sansone was also a partner with Cervantes in Consolidated Service Car Co., a transportation option somewhere between a cab and a bus. Consolidated was the last service car company to operate in the city before accepting a $625,000 deal in 1965 from Bi-State to cease operations.

A devoted Catholic, Sansone chaired the group that oversaw the papal visit to St. Louis by Pope John Paul II. He also chaired the Archdiocese of St. Louis's development appeal for the Catholic Church, and he received the St. Louis King award for dedication to the Catholic faith in St. Louis. In addition to serving on the board of trustees for the Missouri Botanical Garden, he was president of Cardinal Glennon Children's Hospital and the Urological Research Foundation.

In 1970, Sansone founded Huntleigh USA Corp., an airport security firm he later sold. In 1988, the Building and Construction Trades Council named him their "Man of the Year." In 1993, he was one of St. Louis County Executive Buzz Westfall's appointees to the St. Louis County Port Authority. In 1998, the Sansone Group sold many of its shopping centers to a real estate investment trust, opting to focus on managing the properties and marketing them to tenants.

Source: Jacob Barker / *St. Louis Post-Dispatch*, April 28, 2020

Bob Hermann / 1923 – 2020

Bob Hermann was a former St. Louis Man of the Year, Citizen of the Year, and member of the National Soccer Hall of Fame. He was known for his philanthropy and his work on the boards of many civic and charitable organizations including the Muny, the Saint Louis Zoo, and the Missouri Botanical Garden. A big supporter of the St. Louis region, Hermann founded the Veiled Prophet Fair in 1981 as a way to celebrate Independence Day and draw crowds to the Gateway Arch.

Hermann served as a flight deck officer on the *USS Savo Island* aircraft carrier during World War II, seeing action in the southwest Pacific Ocean. He achieved the rank of lieutenant during his time in the U.S. Navy. After graduating from St. Louis Country Day School and Princeton University, he founded Hermann Companies Inc. in 1956. The family-owned business makes plastic containers for food sales, takeout, and delivery, and cling film. Hermann Marketing, another venture, was a pioneer in the fields of promotional marketing and corporate catalog sales before being sold to a company that became part of Staples.

In 1966, Hermann and William D. Cox started what became the National Professional Soccer League. The league quickly merged with the United Soccer Association to form the North American Soccer League. Hermann co-owned the St. Louis Stars team in the NPSL and the NASL from 1967 until the team moved to Anaheim after the 1977 season. He continued as owner of the California Surf until 1980.

The MAC Hermann Trophy, given to the best male and female college soccer players in the country, was funded by him and is named for him. The renovations for the Saint Louis University soccer stadium, now called the Robert R. Hermann Stadium, were largely funded by him.

He was inducted into the National Soccer Hall of Fame in 2001 and the St. Louis Soccer Hall of Fame in 2012.

Hermann and his wife, Mary Lee, were Marlin Perkins Society members for 22 years. He received the prestigious Saint Louis Zoo Award in 1998. Hermann served on the Zoological Park Commission from 1988 to 1998, continuing as Emeritus Commissioner. From 1992 to 1993, he served as Commission Chairman, during which time he created the Zoo Foundation. Hermann served as the Foundation Trustee until 2003, continuing as Emeritus Trustee. In 1999, the Hermann Family Foundation established an endowed fund to create the Hermann Outstanding Employee Awards, which are presented each year to recognize four Zoo employees for exemplary work. The family is recognized at the Hermann Family Grizzly

Hollow at Centene Grizzly Ridge, the large rock in front of The Living World building, the Hermann Foundation at the South Entrance, and the tiger figure on the Mary Ann Lee Conservation Carousel. Hermann is also remembered as the founder of the International Center for Tropical Ecology at the University of Missouri-St. Louis.

Hermann founded the short-lived St. Louis Arts Festival and the Veterans Festival in Forest Park. He also began Operation Brightside, which cleans and beautifies public spaces in the city.

For ten years, he would disappear for a day. Even his family did not know where he went. Later, they found out he would put on a Santa suit and distribute presents to charitable organizations throughout the poorer areas of the region.

Sources: Daniel Neman / *St. Louis Post-Dispatch*; Jeffrey Huntington / *Saint Louis Zoo Magazine*, Summer 2020

Phyllis Schlafly / 1924 – 2016

Phyllis Schlafly was a woman who led the opposition to the Equal Rights Amendment. She was a power broker who could reach a large audience simply by sharing her mailing list. Schlafly was unable to get elected to Congress and was repeatedly shut down from breaking into the St. Louis old boys' clubs. But she managed to go to law school, run a business, and still make dinner in the same day.

When she noticed women resisting the idea of equality (mainly because of the idea of serving in the military), she seized the moment and began her march against an amendment that had bipartisan support. She was concerned that women serving would dilute the military, and she saw the Equal Rights Amendment as a move toward communism.

Schlafly's main method of mobilization was her news-letter called the Phyllis Schlafly Report. Her Rolodex is what helped get Reagan elected and convince the Republican Party to support "pro-life." Donald Trump attended her funeral.

Source: Bruce R. Miller / *Sioux City Journal*, April 9, 2020

Activist Phyllis Schlafly wearing a "Stop ERA" badge, demonstrating with other women against the Equal Rights Amendment in front of the White House, Washington, DC. Photograph by Warren K. Leffler, February 4, 1977.

Madam C. J. Walker / 1867 – 1919

Madam C. J. Walker was America's first self-made female millionaire. Walker, aka Sarah Breedlove, was the first child in her family born into freedom after the 13th Amendment to the Constitution was ratified in 1865. At the beginning of the 20th century, Walker was toiling in St. Louis as a laundress and was dealing with thinning hair. Walker came across homemade balm to mend patchy, broken hair being sold by Annie Malone and became a loyal customer. While Malone was marketing her product as the path to a "lighter, brighter" you, Walker saw an opportunity to cater to the realistic needs of Black women.

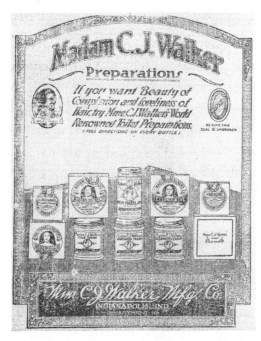

Advertisement showing images of cold cream and hair and complexion products, January 17, 1920. Illustration from *The New York Age*, January 17, 1920 (bound newspaper 10330, Library of Congress Newspaper and Periodicals Reading Room).

Walker eventually built an empire convincing Black women to embrace who they are with her products. Malone and Walker became bitter business rivals. Men were threatened by Walker's power, as Booker T. Washington said, he'd "rather endorse a palm reader than a hair culturist." Walker triumphed to build a groundbreaking business that revolutionized Black hair care and effected social change, opening factories and salons owned and operated by women of color and disrupting the millionaire old boys' club. Her beauty empire revolutionized 20th-century ideals about female enterprise, African American commerce, and beauty standards for women of color.

Source: Lorraine Ali / *Los Angeles Times*, March 25, 2020

Charles Parsons / 1824 – 1905

Charles Parsons is one of St. Louis's most influential yet little-known figures. He was instrumental to the Union cause as a Civil War quartermaster and advisor to generals, politicians, and presidents. As a world-traveling art connoisseur, he helped found the first art museum west of the Mississippi, to which he donated his incredible collection of American, European, and Asian art. His philanthropic work and dedication to education live on in some of the country's grandest institutions.

Portrait of St. Louis banker Charles Parsons taken by noted photographer J. C. Strauss, circa 1895. Parsons was president of the State National Bank, ex-president of the American Bankers Association, and president of the World's Congress of Bankers and Financiers at the Chicago World's Fair of 1893.

Parsons was born in 1824 in upstate New York. In 1864, he settled in St. Louis after his discharge from the Union Army as a lieutenant colonel. In the Army, he served as a quartermaster officer under Gen. William T. Sherman.

Parsons grew wealthy as a St. Louis banker. In 1881, he funded the construction of the first art museum west of the Mississippi: the St. Louis School and Museum of Fine Arts at 19th & Locust streets. His fine art collection can be seen today at the Saint Louis Art Museum and at the Mildred Lane Kemper Art Museum.

In 1896, the *Post-Dispatch* ran an article stating that Parson had funneled $37,500 to the presidential campaign of William McKinley. Parsons denied any such action. Two months later, the *Post-Dispatch* announced that Parsons had been given a seat on the board of directors of the Pulitzer Publishing Co., which owned the newspaper. When he died in 1905, *The St. Louis Republic* remembered Parsons as a "distinguished citizen, venerable banker, art connoisseur, author and philanthropist." Parsons collected Japanese swords, Buddhist statues, and landscapes. He even designed a rear wing at his home at 33 Westmoreland Place to accommodate his art.

Sources: Harry Levins / *St. Louis Post-Dispatch*, February 28, 2020; Amanda Woytus / *St. Louis Magazine*, March 2020

Phyllis Brissenden / 1933 – 2019

Phyllis Brissenden was a philanthropist, theatre life board member, and arts enthusiast. Upon her death, she bequeathed $45 million to the Opera Theatre of Saint Louis. Not only is this the largest gift Opera Theatre of Saint Louis has ever received, it is also one of the largest gifts any American opera company has received.

Brissenden was a music lover who supported Opera Theatre from its first season in 1976. During her lifetime, she contributed roughly $2.5 million to the company. Brissenden led Opera Theatre's National Patrons Council from 2010 – 2017, encouraging opera lovers around the country to support the organization.

She showed the same kindness to volunteers, ushers, and garden staff as she did to star singers. She built lasting relationships with each of the theater's general directors, all of whom remained her lifelong friends. Opera Theatre of Saint Louis dedicated its 2020 production of *Susannah* in memory of Brissenden.

Source: *Webster-Kirkwood Times*

John A. McArthur / 1928 – 2020

John A. McArthur grew up in foster homes and later founded local sporting goods chain Johnny Mac's in 1967. The original location was at the border of Sunset Hills and Crestwood, getting its start in an old doughnut shop before expanding to the building next door. He previously worked for a sporting goods company that went out of business.

Johnny Mac's eventually expanded to operate nine stores across Illinois, Michigan, Indiana, and Missouri, including five in the St. Louis region. McArthur retired in 1985 and passed the business on to his sons.

Area schools and sports leagues depended on Johnny Mac's to supply uniforms and equipment for years. The chain eventually sold part of its business to Dallas-based BSN Sports. Competition from online retailers and big box stores caused Johnny Mac's to close its stores.

McArthur developed and operated the Johnny Mac's Sports Complex in Valley Park after he retired from retail.

Source: Rachel Rice / *St. Louis Post-Dispatch*

Dr. Nicolas N. DeMenil / 1812 – 1882

Dr. Nicolas N. DeMenil arrived here in 1834. He was a physician who opened a drug and chemical store. In 1836, he married Emilie Sophie Chouteau. Emilie was the granddaughter of Pierre Laclede and Marie-Thérèse Chouteau, the city's First Family. Nicolas and Emilie bought a smaller home on the current site of the Chatillon-DeMenil Mansion in the late 1850s before expanding it to create the current house. Marian A. DeMenil, the last DeMenil, died in 2016.

Source: Joe Holleman / *St. Louis Post-Dispatch*, October 19, 2016

The Chatillon-DeMenil House, 3352 South 13th Street, St. Louis, circa 1933. Photograph from the Historic American Buildings Survey collection of the Library of Congress Prints and Photographs Division.

Miss Alma Reitz / 1917 – 2019

Miss Alma Reitz's family-owned Reitz Brothers Stone Company provided much of the stonework in Forest Park among other places around the St. Louis region. In the early 1920s, Alma's grandmother took her and her sister to the Saint Louis Zoo frequently. The fund supports the Zoo's Education Department, helping to provide opportunities to children who may not otherwise enjoy special activities at the Zoo. Alma was honored in 2015 by the St. Louis Planned Giving Council with a Legacy Award for her philanthropy. Through her estate plan, Alma established the Reitz Endowment Fund in memory of her family.

Source: Lori A. Sullivan / *stlzoo*

Fannie Fishman

Fannie Fishman was known as "the only woman bookmaker in the city." She owned and took bets at the St. Charles Cigar Store. She was feisty and smart, dressed in business suits in the 1930s, and and took calls from Vegas, helping to calculate complicated payouts.

In 1928, Fannie divorced Louis Fishman, a racehorse owner. In 1931, the *St. Louis Post-Dispatch* reported that police had arrested Fannie for the fifth time. Many more arrests would follow. In 1941, police had discovered the secret door in the basement, but they still couldn't nab Fannie. She was summoned to testify along with Zeppo Marx in a federal gambling case in Terre Haute, Indiana. She showed up wearing a yellow hat and full polka dot dress with attorney Morris Shenker (Jimmy Hoffa's chief counsel) by her side. When she emerged from the courthouse, her only comment to reporters was that she was retired. "From what?" they asked grinning. "You can say I'm a housewife," she replied.

The next winter, her cigar store was raided again. "Why didn't she just close?" the police captain asked. "I have been here a long time, and if there is a change in things around here, I may be here and you may be gone," she reportedly told him.

In November 1949, a *Post-Dispatch* headline read: "Policemen Outwit Woman Bookie, Seize Evidence." Officers finally were able to grab betting tabs from her hand before she could flush them. The headline a month later read: "Fannie Fishman Freed; Grand Jury Won't Indict Her." In 1952, she finally quit taking bets, but only because of a federal excise tax.

Source: *St. Louis Magazine*, March 2018

W. G. Fienup / 1920 – 2013

Wilbur G. Fienup and his father, William, were the inventors of the spirally wound pop-open biscuit can that led to Pillsbury's Poppin' Fresh DoughBoy. Wilbur, the former president of R.C. Can Co. of St. Louis, died in 2013.

With the fortunes earned from the creation of the famous dough container, Wilbur began purchasing property for his Chesterfield estate in 1968, and in 1972, the house was completed. The more than 223-acre property was used as a farm for many years. The land is now the Fienup Farms development in Chesterfield.

Sources: *Chesterfield Lifestyle magazine*, March 2019; Mary Shapiro / *Out & About*, April – June 2019

Bishop Joseph Rosati / 1789 – 1843

Bishop Joseph Rosati was the driving force behind the building of the Old Cathedral to replace a deteriorating brick church on the riverfront. The Old Cathedral sits upon the only parcel of land in St. Louis that has never changed hands since Pierre Laclede established the village in 1765.

Portrait of Bishop Rosati. Bishop Joseph Rosati (1789 – 1843) served as the first bishop of the Diocese of St. Louis between 1826 and 1843. Among his accomplishments in the St. Louis diocese were the 1828 opening of the St. Louis Hospital, served by the Sisters of Charity, and erecting Saint Louis University in 1829 and the Old Cathedral in St. Louis between 1831 – 1834. From a lantern slide presentation for the 1964 bicentennial of St. Louis's founding in 1764.

He was ordained in 1811, and in 1816, he was recruited for service in America by Louis William DuBourg. Rosati came to America and helped found St. Mary of the Barrens

Seminary in Perryville. A log cabin built in 1818, known as "Rosati's Sacristy," is the oldest building on the campus. Rosati was named as DuBourg's second-in-command in 1823. He became St. Louis's first bishop when St. Louis became a separate diocese in 1826.

Rosati oversaw the creation of what would become DePaul Hospital and Saint Louis University. He was also instrumental in supporting the missionary work of St. Rose Philippine Duchesne.

Rosati was buried in Rome after he died in Europe in 1843. In 1954, Archbishop Joseph E. Ritter petitioned the Vincentians to move Rosati's body to the New Cathedral in St. Louis. In 1971, his remains were moved to the Old Cathedral. Rosati is the only inhabitant of the city's oldest church. Priests at the Old Cathedral knew his remains were below the church, but they weren't sure where until they were discovered by some duct work inspectors.

Rosati served the Diocese of St. Louis from 1827 until his death in 1843.

Source: Joe Holleman / *St. Louis Post-Dispatch*, July 3, 2016

John Hays / 1770 – 1836

John Hays was a civilized, diplomatic, and respected sheriff of St. Clair County. Hays was born around 1770 into a family of Sephardic Jews who fled Spain and emigrated to New York. According to the American Jewish Historical Society, Solomon Hays (John's grandfather) caused one of America's first recorded "shande far di goyim," or scandal in front of the Gentiles, by bringing criminal charges against the Shearith Israel synagogue's (the nation's oldest) board of elders.

As a teenager, John traveled throughout Canada and traded with Native Americans. In 1790, he settled in Cahokia,

Illinois's most populous town at the time. He quickly joined the militia before becoming sheriff of St. Clair County in 1802. John was one of the first Jews to live in Illinois before it became a state. He married a Catholic, but there is no sign that he converted.

John met Lewis and Clark in 1804. His experience with various tribes allowed John to provide military intelligence when he rode out with Ninian Edwards, the Illinois territorial governor, during the War of 1812. (Edwards' sister-in-law was Mary Todd, who married Abe Lincoln.) John moved to Fort Wayne, Indiana, in the 1820s to serve as an agent for the Potawatomi and Miami tribes. In 1823, he returned to Cahokia to retire and become a gentleman farmer. John died in 1836. A plaque honoring Hays was placed at the Cahokia Courthouse in 2019.

Source: *St. Louis Magazine, March 2019*

Robert Wadlow / 1918 – 1940

Robert Wadlow, from Alton, IL, was the tallest man who ever lived and known around the world as the Alton Giant. He measured eight feet and 11.1 inches tall, due to an overactive pituitary gland. He weighed 495 pounds at his heaviest. His furniture, clothing, and car required constant adaptation.

Robert Wadlow intended to study law but instead took a job as a spokesman for Peters Shoe Co., a division of St. Louis's International Shoe Co. He turned down numerous offers from circuses. However, he did appear with The Barnum and Bailey Circus for six days after a financial offer too good to decline.

One pair of his size 37 shoes would cost about $1,500 today. Despite society thinking of him as a "freak," he was gentle, kind, and shy. He happily signed autographs for local children.

Robert visited a family friend's house in Chesterfield every spring for a get-together. Robert passed away in 1940 at age 22 due to a foot infection.

Source: Aimee Pellet / *Chesterfield Lifestyle*, June 2016

Ted Jones / 1925 – 1990

In the 1950s, Edward "Ted" Jones Jr. joined his father, Edward, in the brokerage firm his father started in downtown St. Louis, named Edward Jones. Ted's passion was providing financial advice in the small towns in Missouri's countryside. He discovered a market that others didn't. One of the first Edward Jones offices outside of St. Louis was in Mexico, MO. Ted built a big business from the small-town start and eventually shared ownership of the company with thousands of employees.

He retired in the mid-1980s before focusing on the idea of "rails to trails" in Missouri. In 1986, Ted rode on a bike path in Wisconsin and returned to St. Louis full of excitement for providing Missourians an opportunity to ride and walk through the Missouri countryside, past farm fields and forests and along rivers on a flat, traffic-free trail. At that time, the Missouri Kansas Texas Railroad was abandoning its right-of-way across Missouri. Taking advantage of this great timing, Ted and his wife Pat worked tirelessly for five years to convince landowners, legislators, governors, and the courts that the 280-mile railroad right-of-way should become the Katy Trail. After spending millions of dollars in personal funds and thousands of hours, Ted and Pat cut the ribbon on the first section of trail in 1990. Ted passed away later that year.

After Ted's death, Pat continued to actively support the Katy Trail and countless Missouri-based environmental and conservation organizations. She created Confluence Point State Park, allowing visitors to see the meeting place of the country's two greatest rivers, and donated their family farm to the Missouri Department of Conservation. "Money isn't my goal. I want to spend it on things that are worthwhile," said Ted. "We don't have any children, so we just adopted the state," said Pat.

Source: Dan Burkhardt / *St. Louis Post-Dispatch*, December 31, 2018

Charles Gratiot / 1786 – 1855

Charles Gratiot was born in 1786 and became involved in the fur trade in French Canada. He moved to Cahokia, then St. Louis, and became a prosperous merchant in his 20s. He worked as an interpreter for French, Spanish, and American government officials. Gratiot served as the crowd's translator during the Louisiana Purchase ceremony in 1804.

He was friends with George Rogers Clark and William Clark. He also worked as a translator for Meriwether Lewis. Gratiot married a daughter of Pierre Laclede, Victoire Chouteau, and they had 11 children.

A new north-south road began to develop in the area when Gratiot took ownership of a Spanish land grant in the mid-1780s. The land was called the Gratiot League Square, and it was roughly three miles long on each side. With a western boundary along Big Bend Avenue, the land covered the southern half of Forest Park, The Hill, Dogtown, Hi-Pointe, Clayton-DeMun, Northampton, parts of Richmond Heights, and parts of Maplewood. For easier access and to haul crops, Gratiot laid out three miles of road, 40 feet in width, on his eastern boundary in the 1790s. It ran from his property's northeast point (Euclid Avenue and Barnes Hospital Plaza) to the southeastern point (Pernod Avenue in south St. Louis). Gratiot named it "Rue de Roi," the road of the king. He picked the royal name to charm the local Spanish governor into kicking in some money to help pay for building or maintaining the road. However, Gratiot ended up footing the entire bill. The road was renamed Kingshighway after the Mississippi Valley became part of the U.S. in 1804 during the Louisiana Purchase.

The Gratiot League Square was divided and willed to descendants over the years. Other than a street pronounced "Gratschitt," not much remains to recall Charles Gratiot, a true mover and shaker. His knack for making the right friends and marrying the right woman helped him become a wealthy man.

Source: Joe Holleman / *St. Louis Post-Dispatch*, April 24, 2016

Mary Harris Jones / 1837 – 1930

Mary Harris Jones was known as Mother Jones. A dressmaker by trade, she began fighting for workers' rights around the country after losing her husband and their four children to yellow fever. She possessed the charisma, humor, feistiness, and force of will to organize workers all over the country.

She was buried on December 8, 1930, in the Union Miners Cemetery, the only union-owned cemetery in the country. She asked to be

Mary (Harris) Jones, "Mother Jones," bust portrait, facing left, circa 1902. Photograph from the Library of Congress Prints and Photographs Division.

allowed to "sleep under the clay with those brave boys" after four miners from Mount Olive were killed by hired strikebreakers in 1898. The cemetery is located in Mount Olive, IL, a little coal-mining town that was the center of the struggle to win a living wage in the 1890s. At her funeral, the crowd overflowed the church and people listened to the eulogy through loudspeakers outside in the cold. A large monument was dedicated at Jones's gravesite six years later. The monument includes the names of 22 union members killed in the mine wars of the 1930s, and it has become a gathering spot every year on the historic Miners' Day (October 12th).

"Mother" Jones and her army of striking textile workers beginning their descent on New York. The textile workers of Philadelphia say they intend to show the people of the country their condition by marching through all the important cities. This photograph shows Jones with children and adults beginning their "Children's Crusade" to walk from Philadelphia to Oyster Bay, New York, to publicize the conditions of children working in textile mills. Photograph by Peirce & Jones, 1903.

She once called John D. Rockefeller a "high-class burglar" because "the natural commodities of this country are cornered in the hands of a few."

Her legacy lives on: *Mother Jones Magazine* was established in 1976; Mary Harris "Mother" Jones Elementary School was established in Adelphi, Maryland; The Mother Jones House is an off-campus service house at Wheeling Jesuit University; she was inducted into the National Women's Hall of Fame in 1984; the Annual Mother Jones Festival occurs in Cork City, Ireland; the *Mother Jones and Her Children* documentary premiered in 2014; the *Mother Jones and the Children's Crusade* musical debuted in 2014.

Source: *St. Louis Magazine*, December 2019

Joseph Cromwell Brown / 1784 – 1849

Joseph Cromwell Brown was born in 1784. As a surveyor, he laid down thousands of survey lines and monuments to help shape parts of six states in the Midwest. He was responsible for drawing Missouri's southern and western boundaries and helped document the northern line.

In the 1810s and 1820s, Brown executed the first government-sanctioned surveys of St. Louis. He also served as official county surveyor, St. Louis sheriff, and state senator. Brown was responsible for surveying the Santa Fe Trail from Jackson County, MO, to Taos, NM, and drawing boundaries for treaties with the Osage and Choctaw tribes. The "Honey War" between Iowa and Missouri was prompted by his work in 1837 on trying to better define the existing border. When Iowa farmers living in disputed land refused to pay taxes to Missouri, Missouri revenue collectors chopped down several honey trees in lieu of payment. Opposing state militias eventually met up, with no violence, in the no-man's-land.

It is not clear where Brown is buried, ironic considering he is known for his meticulous documentation of plots of land. The Joseph Cromwell Brown buried at Bellefontaine is actually the surveyor's nephew. A monument dedicated to the surveyor Joseph Cromwell Brown is mistakenly located at the Bellefontaine gravesite. Brown was a member of the Maline Creek Presbyterian Church, located in north St. Louis County near Chambers and Halls Ferry Roads. Some people think he was buried at that cemetery when he died in 1849. The church closed and was abandoned in 1875, which is when people believed his remains were moved to Bellefontaine, which proves to be untrue.

Another theory is that he is buried in Fulton. According to records, Joseph T. Brown, Brown's only son, was a doctor in Fulton and took in his widowed mother.

A surveyor, explorer, adventurer who put Missouri on the map, Brown is one of St. Louis's founding fathers, yet very few people have heard of him.

Source: Joe Holleman / *St. Louis Post-Dispatch*, March 20, 2016

Don Schneeberger / 1930 – 2019

Don Schneeberger owned Vess Beverages for almost 20 years. His father, Leroy Schneeberger, was a salesman for Whistle Orange Co. in 1916 and bought the company (known at that time as Whistle Vess) in 1929. Don started working during the summer for Vess as a teenager in Ladue. He served in the Army and graduated from Washington University with a business degree.

His father sold Vess in 1968, at which point Don had worked his way up to vice president. Don then set up a packaging company before buying back the company in 1975.

Don was also very keen on marketing. At one time, St. Louis was home to three large Vess bottles. One 34-foot steel lemon-lime replica at Sixth & O'Fallon streets downtown still remains.

Vess was churning out 650,000 cases of soda per year when Don bought the company. Two decades later, that had increased to almost 18 million cases.

In 1994, Don sold Vess to Cott Beverages. He then created Merci Water Co., designed houses, and bought multiple businesses in Arizona, where he and his wife had a second home.

Don was a huge fan of St. Louis. He always had a balloon in the Veiled Prophet Parade and was very involved with the Blues and Cardinals. He died on December 27, 2019.

Source: Colleen Schrappen / *St. Louis Post-Dispatch*, December 29, 2019

Eliza Haycraft / 1820 – 1871

Eliza Haycraft arrived in St. Louis by canoe in 1840 after fleeing her home in Callaway County. As the leading brothel madam of the time, she used the Civil War to become very wealthy by servicing both sides of the conflict. One newspaper estimated her estate at $250,000 ($4.7 million today).

Eliza became very philanthropic and supported widows and orphans of Civil War veterans. She was also very famous, as more than 5,000 people attended her funeral and several newspapers covered it.

In April 2014, a state highway work crew uncovered remains of a brick building, likely a warehouse, that Eliza owned near Second & Poplar streets. She owned several brothels and taverns in that area. Despite the fact that she could not read or write, she was smart enough to follow the lead of other businessmen and invested her money in real estate to earn rental income.

Yet her remains are unmarked at Bellefontaine Cemetery. Bellefontaine at that time was the preferred cemetery for St. Louis's elite, yet the cemetery refused to sell her a burial plot. Eliza then suggested it might be better if she met with some of the board of director's wives to discuss the situation. The board relented by offering her a spot at the back end of the cemetery, but only after Eliza agreed to not install a monument or headstone. She eventually bought a premium lot large enough to accommodate 20 bodies. A "Civil War 27" signpost marks the site (to help visitors on guided tours). Eliza's burial plot ended up near the front of the cemetery as the main entrance to the cemetery switched from being off Broadway to being off West Florissant in the 1930s. Eliza has some distant relatives in Louisiana, but they have no interest in pushing for a headstone.

Source: Joe Holleman / *St. Louis Post-Dispatch*, May 22, 2016

Joan Blasé Goodson / 1926 – 2020

Joan Blasé Goodson was a philanthropist and founding board member of the Contemporary Art Museum. She graduated from Kirkwood High School in 1943. After college, she returned to St. Louis to become an advertising copywriter and publicist. She married Jean S. Goodson in 1962 and moved to his large property on Des Peres Road. Despite selling off parcels for subdivisions over time, they retained over 40 acres. They donated 10 acres to the Missouri Department of Conservation in 1997. The donated land is now known as Bittersweet Woods (Goodson loved the bittersweet flavor) and is maintained by the City of Des Peres. The Goodsons built a modest midcentury modern house, designed by Ted Berger, a St. Louis architect. They loved to entertain on their property with horses, hayrides, sleigh rides, fishing, ice skating, cats, dogs, chickens, goats, and Mexican burros.

Jean was the president of the International Hat Company. The property included a row of small houses, which the Goodsons rented to local secondary school teachers.

Joan supported the Opera Theatre of Saint Louis, St. Louis Chamber Chorus, Saint Louis Art Museum, St. Louis Symphony Orchestra, Repertory Theatre St. Louis, Frank Lloyd Wright House, Landmarks Association, and the Missouri Botanical Garden.

Source: Sarah Bryan Miller / *St. Louis Post-Dispatch*, June 7, 2020

Joseph Pulitzer / 1847 – 1911

Joseph Pulitzer emigrated to St. Louis from Hungary. Once in

Joseph Pulitzer at 40. Head and shoulders, arms crossed, facing left, glasses, beard. 1924

St. Louis, he drove mules, hauled baggage, waited tables, and read English and law books at the Mercantile Library.

At age 31, he purchased the *St. Louis Post-Dispatch*. At age 36, he purchased the *New York World*. He won over the New Yorkers by being colorful, intelligent, and socially conscious. Joseph urged his reporters to seek "what is original, dramatic, romantic, odd, and apt to be talked about." By age 43, he was incredibly sensitive to noise and nearly blind, some say from him working too hard. He used an elaborate, confidential codebook to run his papers from soundproofed rooms on his yacht in Bar Harbor, Maine.

His bequest established the Columbia School of Journalism, where in 1917, the first Pulitzer Prize was awarded.

Source: *St. Louis Magazine*, April 2019

Jack the Ripper / Died 1903

Jack the Ripper terrorized the streets of East London in the second half of 1888 by killing and mutilating women. This was known as the "The Whitechapel Murders." Some evidence points to Jack the Ripper being Dr. Francis J. Tumblety. Tumblety left Rochester, NY, and came to St. Louis in 1863. In the 1870s, he moved to New York City. He used New York City as a base for traveling. One trip included a visit to London in June 1888. The "Ripper murders" included Mary Ann Nichols, Annie Chapman, and Catherine Eddowes. Organs had been removed from Chapman and Eddowes. Tumblety was arrested in London for "gross indecency," a term used to denote homosexual activity at the time. He was released on November 8. On November 9, Mary Kelly was grossly murdered by Jack the Ripper, with her heart and uterus being removed. Tumblety was arrested on suspicion of the murders on November 12, but he was released without being charged. He eventually made his way back to New York.

It was told that in 1861, during a dinner party in Washington, DC, Tumblety showed guests specimen jars that held human uteruses and referred to women as "cattle." Richard Norris, a lover of Tumblety's when he would visit during Mardi Gras, said that Tumblety invited Norris to his hotel room to seduce him. While he was there, Tumblety showed Norris a collection of knives and surgical instruments.

In the last years of his life, Tumblety moved between Baltimore, New Orleans, and St. Louis. He checked himself into St. John's Hospital in downtown St. Louis and died there on May 28, 1903.

Source: Joe Holleman / *St. Louis Post-Dispatch*, February 5, 2017

Pleasant E. Devinney / 1818 – 1895

Pleasant E. Devinney was born in 1818 in Alabama to William and Nancy Brooster Devinney. He arrived in St. Louis in 1828. By 1852, he was a successful steamboat captain. He invested in the *Twin City*, one of the largest stern-wheelers at the time. The *Twin City* carried cargo from Pittsburg to St. Louis for the next three years. It was moored in St. Louis in 1855, where a fire broke out and destroyed the ship.

Devinney married Priscilla Long in 1856. Priscilla was the granddaughter of Lawrence Long, a Chesterfield pioneer, and widow of Reuben Long, her first cousin.

Also in 1856, the Pacific Railroad Packet Line was established. It was used to carry supplies and mail to government forts along the Missouri River. Six elegant steamers composed the line by 1858, and Captain Devinney became the master of the *St. Mary*. *St. Mary* was known for its incredible speed and accommodations.

Devinney was also a landowner and farmer in Chesterfield. In 1877, Devinney acquired an additional 130 acres of land. This included the western portion of the original town of Chesterfield (as platted by Justus Post) that Devinney purchased from his stepdaughter Amanda, who inherited the land from her father Reuben Long. Devinney purchased the property, located along Wild Horse Creek Road between Baxter and Wilson Roads, for $1,200.

Devinney's son, Pleasant, married Hattie Lee Payne. Dolly Lee, their daughter, inherited all of Devinney's land holdings in Chesterfield as she was his only grandchild. A 1909 St. Louis County map denoted the property as Dolly Devinney.

Focused on preserving history, Captain Devinney became a charter member of the Old Settlers Association of St. Louis

County in 1887, where he attended meetings at the St. Louis County Fairgrounds. He died in 1895 in Glendale, MO, and is buried in Bellefontaine Cemetery.

Source: Ann Chrissos / *Out & About*, January – March 2017

David R. Francis / 1850 – 1927

David R. Francis graduated from Washington University at age 20. He was elected St. Louis mayor in 1885, at age 35, after relinquishing a lucrative career as a commodities broker. At age 38, he became the youngest governor in the nation after he was elected governor of Missouri in 1889. He is the only person to serve as both St. Louis mayor and Missouri governor. From 1896 – 1897,

David R. Francis, half length, facing left, circa 1903. Photograph from the Library of Congress Prints and Photographs Division.

Francis served as U.S. Secretary of the Interior.

He was the President of the 1904 World's Fair Louisiana Purchase Exposition. Francis Field at Washington University is named in his honor. In 1916, Francis became the U.S. ambassador to Russia.

In 1916 on Christmas Eve, Francis went into City Hall dressed as Santa Claus and donated 60 acres of land in the southwest section of the city. That land became Francis Park in St. Louis Hills. A seven-foot-tall, 900-pound statue of Francis now stands at the park.

Source: Joe Holleman / *St. Louis Post-Dispatch, February 26, 2017*

Vincent Leonard Price Jr. / 1911 – 1993

Vincent Clarence Price was a New York pharmacist and homeopath in the 1850s. He used his skills to create the world's first cream of tartar baking powder to help his mother reinvent her leaden biscuits. He then went west to sell it. Shortly after, Price was selling fine extracts of vanilla and lemon, breakfast cereal, and even dog food.

After the stock market crashed, Price pulled his youngest son, Vincent Leonard Price, out of Yale to help save one family business, the National Candy Company. Vincent Leonard moved to St. Louis in 1902 after real-

Portrait of Vincent Price, in "Angel Street," captured by Carl Van Vechten, November 11, 1942.

izing it would be the host for the Olympics and World's Fair. The business was soon one of the biggest candy companies in the country.

Vincent Leonard Jr. was born in 1911 and was christened the Candy Kid by the Candymaker's Association. Vincent Leonard Jr. attended attended St. Louis Country Day School and Yale where he studied art history. By this time, Vincent Leonard Sr. had had specialized in penny candy, making a fortune with affordable candy during the next stock market crash. Vincent Leonard Jr. next studied art at the University of London before performing on the London stage. At six-foot-four with refined elegance, Vincent Leonard Jr. eventually made a career out of playing roles of suave, likable Gothic villains and starring in horror movies. He was an art collector (he bought a Rembrandt at age 12) and was very interested in culture and food. He even wrote three cookbooks.

Source: *St. Louis Magazine*, October 2018

Marguerite Martyn / 1878 – 1948

Marguerite Martyn was a *Post-Dispatch* columnist in the early 20th century. She was known for her ability to illustrate her subjects in pen and ink. She was sent from her home in Springfield, MO, to study art at Washington University by her widowed mother. Martyn designed jewelry and opened art studios after graduation.

Post-Dispatch newsroom management became aware of her skills when she submitted unsolicited drawings of the St. Louis World's Fair for publication. She was hired in 1905, and the paper's editor, O. K. Bovard, quickly pushed her into writing. At a time when women in newsrooms were a minority, she was able to choose her own assignments. Martyn interviewed everyday people, first ladies, suffragists, governors, and presidents, sketching them as they talked. These illustrations generally accompanied her articles. Readers would note that Martyn had included a small self-portrait in the sketches, showing herself sketching the interviewee. She interviewed residents of Westmoreland Place and covered the city's illegal "Lid Clubs," where illicit and underage drinking took place on Sundays. Martyn traveled to Jefferson City to report on the suffragists' lobbying of the all-male Missouri Legislature.

She married Clair Kenamore, a *Post-Dispatch* editor, in 1913. Kenamore moved to Arizona in 1931 and died of tuberculosis in 1935 in Oregon. Martyn continued living in Webster Groves while she worked for the newspaper. She died in 1948 at age 68 and is buried in Kirkwood at Oak Hill Cemetery.

Source: Frank Absher / *St. Louis Post-Dispatch*, March 10, 2019

Kenneth McKenzie / 1797 – 1861

Kenneth McKenzie was a fur trader who once owned the land that became a 12-acre village known as MacKenzie. In total, he owned 3,000 acres between River des Peres and what is now Laclede Station Road.

McKenzie was born in Scotland in 1797. He came to America as a young man and became president of the Columbia Fur Co., which eventually merged with American Fur Co. McKenzie became known as the "Emperor of the West" and the "King of the Missouri." He liked to entertain guests by serving fresh buffalo meat and iced wines at Fort Union, which he built in an area that is now North Dakota. The pelts collected by his trappers were sent back to St. Louis via steamboat and distributed to East Coast cities. He expanded the trade by deciding to send steamboats *up* the river. McKenzie built a still and made Indian corn whiskey to help him and his men get through the long winters and compete with other traders. Federal law prohibited liquor at the forts, and when officials got wind of the operation, McKenzie was sharply rebuked.

In 1834, he retired from fur trading and learned to make wine in Europe. After making his way back to St. Louis, he began to import fine wines and liquors. McKenzie married and had four children, including a son whom he had with a Native American woman at Fort Union.

He invested in land and railroads. He was adventuresome, ruthless, competitive, and had a taste for the finer things. McKenzie died at age 64 in 1861 and is buried in Bellefontaine Cemetery. The village of Mackenzie (there is not a good explanation as to why the spelling changed) was developed in the 1930s and officially incorporated in 1946. Mackenzie Road is also named after him.

Source: Valerie Schremp Hahn / St. Louis Post-Dispatch, March 17, 2019

James Jennings / 1781 – 1855

James Jennings was a Virginia merchant and farmer who moved to a large property north of St. Louis in 1839. He moved to the area with his wife, Anne, seven children, and roughly 30 slaves. Nobody is certain why Jennings decided to come to St. Louis, but the best explanation to date is that the St. Louis mayor at the time, Dr. William Carr Lane, was a college friend.

His 2,500-acre property encompassed most of the current Jennings boundaries, plus Floridell Hills and Country Club Hills. Jennings' slaves built a 23-room, three-story mansion on College Avenue and what is now Oepts Avenue. Jennings raised crops on the property and sold hay at a market in downtown St. Louis.

Jennings died at age 74 in 1855 from consumption and is buried in Bellefontaine Cemetery. Until 1900, his mansion was used as the St. Louis Seminary for Young Women. In 1923, a fire destroyed the building. In 1946, the city of Jennings was incorporated. A plaque marking the estate is installed in a retaining wall at Hord & Blewett Avenues.

McLaran and Switzer Avenues are named after Jennings' sons-in-law. Ada Wortley Avenue is named after a great-granddaughter who died of bronchitis when she was five years old.

Source: Valerie Schremp Hahn / *St. Louis Post-Dispatch*, March 17, 2019

The Collins Brothers

The Collins family arrived from Connecticut in what is now known as Collinsville, IL, in the 1810s. The five brothers (Augustus, Anson, William, Michael, and Frederick) were very active, energetic businessmen with ample capital.

The brothers bought the log cabin of John Cook in 1818. Cook was a Virginia man who had built the first permanent home in the area in 1810. They built a distillery, sawmill, and flour mill.

They originally wanted to name the area Unionville. They decided on Collinsville after learning that Illinois already had a Unionville once a post office was established in 1825.

The distillery was successful, but they gave it up during the temperance movement of the 1820s. William remained in the area to operate a mill, farm, and general store. Michael and Frederick moved away, and Augustus and Anson died. A trunk, photographs, fans, and other items from the Collins family are located at the Collinsville Historical Museum. The town's first cemetery was established on land donated by William Collins. He is buried there with his parents and other family members.

The oldest house in Collinsville, built in 1845, is believed to be the D. D. Collins House, which sits in Collins Park. D. D. Collins is likely not related to the Collins brothers.

Source: Valerie Schremp Hahn / *St. Louis Post-Dispatch*, March 17, 2019

Benjamin Godfrey / 1794 – 1862

Benjamin Godfrey, a ship captain, merchant, and investor, was born in Chatham, Massachusetts. When he was nine years old, he went to sea with his stepfather. He spent some time in Ireland before serving in the War of 1812 with the American Navy. As the head of a merchant vessel, he sailed the world.

During this time, he made business connections that allowed him to start a shipping firm in Alton, IL. A stone warehouse was built by him and his business partner at William Street and West Broadway. This is the same warehouse where newspaper editor Elijah Lovejoy would later be killed while protecting his press.

Godfrey Homestead, Delhi Road, Godfrey, Madison County, IL, circa 1933. Photograph from the Historic American Buildings Survey collection of the Library of Congress Prints and Photographs Division.

St. Paul's Episcopal Church, the first church in Alton, was built by Godfrey. Because he believed women should have a formal education, Godfrey established the Monticello Female Seminary. The school is now the site of Lewis and Clark Community College. The first railroad in Madison County, which led to Springfield, Illinois, was built with the help of Godfrey.

Godfrey was a family man, a religious man, a gentleman, a visionary, an entrepreneur, the namesake of Godfrey, Illinois, and a founding father of the Alton area. He died in 1862 and is buried in Godfrey Cemetery. The North Alton-Godfrey Business Council dedicated seven historical markers related to Godfrey's life.

Source: Valerie Schremp Hahn / *St. Louis Post-Dispatch*, March 17, 2019

Ninian Edwards / 1775 – 1833

From 1809 to 1818, Ninian Edwards was the governor of the Illinois Territory. He also served in various leadership roles until he became Illinois's third governor.

Thomas Kirkpatrick was the area's first European settler. He built a log cabin overlooking Cahokia Creek on what is now the north side of Edwardsville. Edwards named the cabin as the county seat for the newly formed Madison County in 1812. In return, Kirkpatrick named the area Edwardsville in 1813.

Edwards built a home on what is now the site of the convent at St. Boniface Catholic Church, on the corner of Fillmore & East Vandalia Streets. One of his sons, Albert Gallatin Edwards, founded A. G. Edwards & Co. in 1887 in St. Louis.

Ninian Edwards died of cholera in 1833 in Belleville. He is buried in Oak Grove Cemetery in Springfield, near the tomb of president Abraham Lincoln. Another son, named Ninian also, was the brother-in-law of Mary Todd Lincoln's sister, Elizabeth.

The plaza in downtown Edwardsville contains a statue of Edwards.

Source: Valerie Schremp Hahn / *St. Louis Post-Dispatch*, March 17, 2019

Menlo Smith / Born 1927

Before he was school age, Menlo Smith's family moved from Arizona to Texas to Colorado to Utah. He swept floors in his father's shop for pocket money, served in three branches of the military, earned a business degree, and raised five children with Mary Jean, his first wife.

In Utah during the Depression, Smith's father had been out of work and tried door-to-door sales. One of the items he sold was a sugary drink that he mixed and packaged himself, similar to Kool-Aid. Smith's father named the product Fruzola. During World War II, penny candy became hard to come by due to sugar rations. One-cent sugar pouches became very popular with children. They would lick their fingers and dip them in the powder for a sugar buzz.

Edwards Place, a famous historic mansion in Springfield, Illinois. The house was built in 1833 in the Greek Revival style, and several revisions created the Italianate house preserved today. Lawyer Benjamin S. Edwards, son of Illinois governor Ninian Edwards, owned the house, which became an important political center, hosting rallies for both Abraham Lincoln and his famous debate opponent, Stephen A. Douglas. Some Lincoln family possessions are held in the Edwards house. Photograph from the Carol M. Highsmith Archive of the Library of Congress Prints and Photographs Division.

At age 17, Smith had no interest in the candy business, originally wanting to be a dentist, and he joined the Army. He later enrolled in the University of Utah. Eventually noticing the potential of the product, he made a move.

In the mid-20th century, 25-year-old Menlo Smith moved from Utah to University City with his wife and two toddlers. He was attracted to the area due to its central location and the minimal cost of raw materials.

At this time, he possessed the recipe for Fruzola. In 1952, Smith opened the Fruzola Company of St. Louis in a warehouse on Olive Street in Midtown. Just three years later, sales of Lik-M-Aid, the precursor to Fun Dip, had topped $1 million. The candy demand from young baby boomers caused the business to expand rapidly. As popular as it was, Lik-M-Aid was seen primarily as a drink mix, not a candy. Vendors wanted to stock it only in the summer. So Smith repackaged the same powder inside a colorful straw, which became Pixy Stix in 1959. Mothers thought the Pixy Stix were too messy, so in 1963 Smith ran the Pixy Stix powder through the presses at the TUMS antacid factory in downtown St. Louis. This became a SweeTART.

Through acquisitions and partnerships, the company, at this time known as Sunline, was responsible for creating Sprees, Scrunch Bars, Scrumdiddlyumptious, Oompas, Everlasting Gobstoppers, Runts, and Bottle Caps. Under a new parent company, Sunset Hills–based Sunmark Corp., the business was selling 87 million pounds of confections a year. At its height, the company ran 10 plants and had 1,500 employees. In 1982, the company was doing $122 million in sales.

Smith decided to step away from the business to spend three years on a Mormon Church mission in the Philippines. He eventually decided to focus his time on venture capitalism. By 1986, he was ready to get out of the sugar business.

Rountree Mackintosh purchased Sunmark. Nestlé acquired Rountree before closing Sunmark's corporate offices in 1999. The last two candy plants, both located in Affton, were closed in 2006.

Fun Dip, Pixy Stix, SweeTARTS, Sprees, and Nerds all sprouted from the original Fruzola pouch of powder. St. Louis was home to the number four nonchocolate confectioner in the U.S.

In his middle-age years, Smith took up heli-skiing and off-road Jeeping, converted to Mormonism, and launched a nonprofit that offered microloans in developing nations. He helped establish the St. Louis Missouri Temple of the Church of Jesus Christ of Latter-day Saints. He also completed a 300-page memoir about how a boy born in "a little place you've never heard of" became a real-life Willy Wonka. The Chesterfield resident is known to ride his bicycle every morning and volunteer at his church. After he was widowed in 2011, he married his former executive secretary, Kathryn.

Source: Colleen Schrappen / *St. Louis Post-Dispatch*, November 24, 2019

George Herbert Walker / 1875 – 1953

George Herbert Walker, who was known as Bert, was born in 1875 as the only child of David Davis "D. D." Walker and Martha Adela Beaky. D. D. Walker was the founder of Ely & Walker Dry Goods Co., the largest wholesaler of dry goods west of the Mississippi. The landmark downtown warehouse is now loft condominiums.

In 1897, Bert graduated from Washington University. While at school, he won the Missouri heavyweight boxing championship.

In 1900, he launched G. H. Walker & Co., a banking and investment firm with offices nationwide. Bert far exceeded his father's fortune, building a financial empire that would bankroll generations. Bert helped organize the 1904 World's Fair. He was the president of the United States Golfing Association. He also helped establish the school that would become MICDS, the Racquet Club, and golf's Walker Cup.

Bert had six children with his wife, Lucretia Walker. In 1901, their daughter Dorothy was born. The family lived in a

15-room Italian Renaissance mansion at 12 Hortense Place in the Central West End. When Dorothy was 18, she was introduced to Prescott Bush, a recent Yale graduate and star athlete from Ohio. Prescott had just moved to St. Louis and was making $100 a month selling tools. With Bert's blessing, Prescott proposed marriage in 1920.

The Ely & Walker Dry Goods Company warehouse, at 2132 O'Fallon, is visible in the right background. Photographed by Richard W. Lemen, June 18, 1930.

Bert moved to New York to become president of W. A. Herriman & Co. bank. Prescott went on to a career on Wall Street, and from 1952 to 1963, he served as a U.S. senator from Connecticut.

Prescott and Dorothy had a son, George H. W., and grandson, George W., who would both go on to the White House. In 1902, D. D. bought land and built a mansion on what is now Walker's Point, Maine (where the Bush family still vacations). William H. T. "Bucky" Bush, born in Greenwich, Connecticut,

61

was George H. W. Bush's youngest brother. Bucky reestablished his family's presence in St. Louis as he was co-founder and chairman of Clayton-based Bush O'Donnell Investment Advisors Inc. He sat on the board of directors for Maritz Inc. and was chairman of the board for Saint Louis University, the Missouri Botanical Garden, and The Muny. Bucky died in West Palm Beach in 2018, at the age of 79. Another grandson of Bert's, George Herbert Walker III, made St. Louis his home.

Source: Jeremy Kohler / *St. Louis Post-Dispatch*, December 2, 2018

George Herbert Walker III / 1932 – 2020

George Herbert "Bert" Walker III was a civic leader and philanthropist. He grew up in Greenwich, Connecticut. He served in the Air Force in the mid-1950s after earning an undergraduate degree from Yale and a law degree from Harvard.

Walker III moved to St. Louis in 1958 to work for the financial firm founded by his grandfather. After his father, George Herbert Walker Jr., named an outsider as his successor, Walker III found a new career at Stifel, Nicolaus in 1976 before becoming chairman and CEO of the Stifel, Nicolaus and Co. brokerage firm.

He was a cousin of George H. W. Bush. Their grandfather was George Herbert Walker, who founded a banking and investment firm with offices nationwide.

Walker III was active in Missouri Republican politics. He ran unsuccessfully for the GOP nomination for the U.S. House from the 2nd District in 1992. He was U.S. ambassador to Hungary from 2003 to 2006 in the George W. Bush administration. Walker III chaired a committee that successfully passed a statewide constitutional amendment in 2002 to allow St. Louis to make changes in the city's county-type elected offices. Two years later, city voters rejected a follow-up proposal to make such offices appointive. He was the initial chairman of the Better Together organization, which proposed a plan to merge the city and St. Louis County.

Walker III served on the Webster University board for 42 years, including six as the chairman. The Webster business school was renamed in his honor after his $10 million donation in 2005. He funded the Walker Leadership Institute, a partnership between Webster University and Eden Theological Seminary to bring together business and faith leaders and students. Walker III chaired the Missouri Historical Society and Downtown St. Louis Inc. boards. He served on the Saint Louis Science Center commission and the board of the Urban League of Metropolitan St. Louis.

He married three times but remained close with his children and 15 grandchildren. He was known as being strong, polite, cheerful, and elegant. Walker III died in 2020 at the age of 88.

Source: Mark Schlinkmann / *St. Louis Post-Dispatch*, January 22, 2020

John Ball / 1779 – 1859

James Ball, John's father, came to America from Dublin and served in the Revolutionary War. James was a friend of Daniel Boone.

In the late 1700s, John Ball moved to west St. Louis County and bought 400 acres along Grand Glaize Creek. In 1826, Jefferson City was established as the state capital. People needed an overland route to get mail to Jefferson City from St. Louis. Therefore, a road, eventually becoming Manchester Road, was built that happened to go by Ball's property.

Ball laid out a town and originally named the area "Ballshow." Two days later, he renamed it "Ballwin." A great-grandson said that because of the town's rivalry with more prominent and nearby Manchester, Ball was certain his town would "win" out in growth and reputation. In 1859, Ball died at age 79. His and his wife's remains are located at Manchester Methodist Cemetery. His homestead is now the site of a Regions Bank, and a historic marker sits on the bank's front lawn at 14915 Manchester Road.

Source: Valerie Schremp Hahn / *St. Louis Post-Dispatch*, February 3, 2019

Harry Innes Bodley / 1804 – 1883

As the head of the First Family of Kirkwood, Harry Innes Bodley is the founding father of Kirkwood. Bodley was elected as president of the Kirkwood Association. In 1853, he established a 40-block plat known as the Town of Kirkwood.

In addition to being a civic leader and town founder, he was also an insurance man and minister. He held Episcopalian services just outside the Kirkwood city limits at his Homewood home. His following grew to the point where they needed to build a church. Bodley was one of the founders of the original Grace Episcopal Church, located where Eliot Chapel currently sits at Taylor & Argonne.

Among many notable in-laws and descendants was B. Gratz Brown. Brown was in a famous gun duel on Bloody Island that left him permanently impaired. He eventually became governor of Missouri. Henry Hough, for which Hough Elementary (Kirkwood School District) was named, was also a relative. Abram S. Mitchell, who left Kirkwood to write editorials against the Civil War for the *New York Times*, was married to Judith Bodley.

Source: Don Corrigan / *Webster-Kirkwood Times*, April 29 – May 5, 2016

Robert A. Barnes / 1808 – 1892

Robert A. Barnes was born in Washington, DC in 1808. His father died when Barnes was 13 years old. moved to Louisville, KY, to live with his uncle, who was a merchant and taught him the rules of business.

Barnes moved to St. Louis in 1830, where he took a job as a clerk. He was paid $25 a month and was allowed to sleep in the store. He saved what he could and placed it in an interest-bearing account, to the point where he was able to start buying and selling things on his own. In 1836, he was clerking in a grocery. The following year, he was made a partner due to his skill and work ethic.

In 1840, he became a director of the Bank of the State of Missouri. Eighteen years later, he became the bank president.

When Adolphus Busch was looking for a loan to expand his father-in-law's brewery, every other bank in town turned him down. As president of the bank, Barnes decided to loan Busch $50,000. Busch would never forget this, and he donated millions to Barnes Hospital.

In 1845, he married Louise DeMun, a descendant of the Chouteau family. Both of their children died in infancy. Louise died in 1889. Barnes died in 1892 at his St. Louis residence at 521 Garrison near Washington Avenue. He is buried at Bellefontaine Cemetery.

After leaving small amounts to various relatives and business associates, most of his estate was left to charitable organizations. One million dollars of that estate was designated for a hospital. Trustees of the estate realized this was not enough money for what Barnes wanted, so the money was invested. By 1912, the endowment was worth $2 million, and land was purchased near Forest Park. The architect of

Union Station, Theodore Link, was hired to design the hospital complex. Washington University agreed to make it the school's teaching hospital. Barnes Hospital opened in 1914 with 250 beds. In 1996, Barnes and Jewish would merge to become Barnes-Jewish Hospital.

The Martin F. Hanley House at 7600 Westmoreland Drive, Clayton, St. Louis County. The oldest building in the county seat of St. Louis County. Built in 1855 on what was then a 112-acre farm, the house has survived without major changes as a new city of 15,000 population has grown up around it. Mr. and Mrs. Hanley gave a four-acre strip of land to help establish the village of Clayton when it was founded in 1878. Hanley Road, now a major street, was originally laid out as the access lane bordering the farm on the west. The Hanley house is unusual in having survived without major change and with its two-storied wood gallery extending full length along the west (rear) elevation and with the separate brick one-story wing related to it. Illustration from the Historic American Buildings Survey collection of the Library of Congress Prints and Photographs Division.

Martin Hanley / 1814 – 1879

Martin Hanley was a farmer from Virginia. During the divorce of St. Louis and St. Louis County in 1876, officials needed a place to establish their courthouse. Along with the 100 acres from Ralph Clayton, Hanley donated four acres, mostly to have his name attached to the donation. He built a two-story farmhouse in 1855. This house still stands and is currently a museum. The village of Hanley Hills and Hanley Road are named for Hanley.

Source: Valerie Schremp Hahn / *St. Louis Post-Dispatch*, February 3, 2019

Ralph Clayton / 1788 – 1883

Ralph Clayton was a farmer from Virginia. During the divorce of St. Louis and St. Louis County in 1876, officials needed a place to establish their courthouse. Clayton convinced government officials this his land was a more central spot than Kirkwood and Mount Olive, the other areas they considered. His land was "half a day's ride from the city," Clayton said.

In return for naming the area after him, Clayton donated 100 acres, which makes up most of the present-day Clayton business district. In 1878, Clayton offered a prayer and dug the first dirt for the courthouse. Both of Clayton's homes, a brick home and a log cabin, burned in fires.

Source: Valerie Schremp Hahn / *St. Louis Post-Dispatch*, February 3, 2019

James P. Kirkwood / 1807 – 1877

James P. Kirkwood was a Scottish civil engineer. In the 1850s, he was the superintendent of the Missouri Pacific Railroad and was in charge of locating and building the railroad. In 1853, Kirkwood became the first planned suburb west of the Mississippi River.

Kirkwood left the area to be in charge of water resources and aqueducts in cities around the country, but he returned to St. Louis to work on pumping stations. The city's first major water treatment plant at Bissell's Point, now the location of a present-day plant, was built by Kirkwood.

He moved to New York and died there in 1877. He is the namesake of Kirkwood, MO and Kirkwood, NY. A historic marker is dedicated to him at the Kirkwood train station.

Source: Valerie Schremp Hahn / *St. Louis Post-Dispatch*, February 3, 2019

Theodore Kimm / 1811 – 1886

Theodore Kimm was a German immigrant and dry goods merchant from St. Louis. The cholera epidemic and the great St. Louis fire of 1849, which destroyed the riverfront's warehouse district, prompted him to leave the city.

Kimm founded Kimmswick, an area that gained notoriety in 1839 when a mastodon skeleton was found there. In 1859, Kimm laid out the town's first five blocks. He became the first postmaster and added the suffix "wick," which means settlement or town, to the name.

In retirement, Kimm and his wife, Wilhelmine, traveled throughout Europe. He died in Switzerland and is buried there. His wife and son Ernest, who died at nine years old, are buried in Kimmswick.

Source: Valerie Schremp Hahn / *St. Louis Post-Dispatch*, February 3, 2019

William Lindsay Long / 1789 – 1849

After a major wave of settlers arrived in the area in the 1770s, William Lindsay Long founded Fenton in 1818. He named the town after his grandmother, Elizabeth Fenton Bennett.

In 1833, a ferry and post office were built, which attracted more people to the town. In 1854, the first bridge was built across the river by a group of businessmen.

Long's wife, Elizabeth Sappington, was the sister of Thomas Sappington. Thomas Sappington was the original owner of Sappington House in Crestwood. The Longs built their first home, which was later owned by Ulysses S. Grant, known as "White Haven." Long moved to Fenton after selling White Haven. He eventually moved back near White Haven, where he built a log home that currently stands along Pardee Road and is owned by the county.

His son, John Fenton Long, became a police chief and judge in St. Louis. Long is buried in Sappington Cemetery.

Source: Valerie Schremp Hahn / *St. Louis Post-Dispatch*, February 3, 2019

South front and east side of the William Long Log House, 9385 Pardee Road, Crestwood, St. Louis County. Photograph from the Historic American Buildings Survey collection of the Library of Congress Prints and Photographs Division.

East front elevation of the Thomas Sappington House, Sappington Road, Crestwood, St. Louis County. Photograph by Paul Piaget, April 1960.

William B. Ferguson / 1814 – 1911

William B. Ferguson came to the area from Ohio. He bought some land and, in 1855, deeded part of it as a right-of-way for a railroad. The one stipulation was that they name the train station after him.

Side facade showing end chimney of the Ferguson Log Cabin, 3631 Brown Road, Overland, St. Louis County. Photograph from the Historic American Buildings Survey collection of the Library of Congress Prints and Photographs Division.

After Ferguson returned from fighting in the Civil War, he started to lay out streets and selling property to farmers. In 1876, a spur line linking Ferguson to downtown St. Louis was built, causing the town to grow into a rail suburb. In 1894, the city was incorporated.

A real estate investor and civic leader, Ferguson donated the land for the first Presbyterian church in the Ferguson, MO, area. Eventually, he moved to California, where he died at age 97 in 1911.

Source: Valerie Schremp Hahn / *St. Louis Post-Dispatch*, February 3, 2019

John O'Fallon / 1791 – 1865

John O'Fallon was an Army captain, a whiskey maker, a Missouri state representative, a bank president, and a railroad president. Known as being a generous man, he donated land for Saint Louis University and Washington University. His country estate became O'Fallon Park in St. Louis.

Portrait of John O'Fallon. John O'Fallon (1791 – 1865) was a St. Louis military man, merchant, and philanthropist who founded the O'Fallon Polytechnic Institute in St. Louis. Image from a lantern slide presentation for the 1964 bicentennial of St. Louis's founding in 1764.

Brothers Nicholas and Arnold Krekel founded a town in Missouri and named it after John O'Fallon because of his railroad's contribution to the area's growth. Nicholas Krekel's house still sits across from city hall and faces the railroad.

O'Fallon, IL, was originally known as O'Fallon Station, also named after John O'Fallon. In 1854, O'Fallon Station was built, a water tank was built, and city lots were platted and sold.

John O'Fallon was the nephew of explorer William Clark. He died in 1865 and is buried in Bellefontaine Cemetery.

Source: Valerie Schremp Hahn / *St. Louis Post-Dispatch*, February 3, 2019

Tom Bullock / 1873 – 1964

Tom Bullock was a famed pre-Prohibition African American bartender. He was the author of *The Ideal Bartender*. Bullock established his reputation while working at the St. Louis Country Club. He is known to have invented the Clover Leaf cocktail. A fan of juleps and fizz cocktails, Bullock was very influential in the bar and cocktail movement in St. Louis.

Source: Kevin C. Johnson / *St. Louis Post-Dispatch*, July 3 – 9, 2020

Members of the executive committee of the Pageant and Masque stand on the drama's set. Several prominent citizens served on the committee for the civic drama held in Forest Park, May 1914. Officers were John H. Gundlach, chairman; Henry W. Barth, vice chair; Luther Ely Smith, secretary; Benjamin J. Taussig, treasurer; and Charlotte Rumbold, executive secretary. Other committee members were Dwight F. Davis, Arthur E. Bostwick, Mrs. Philip N. Moore, William LaBeaume, Charles A. Stix, F. H. Smith, George W. Simmons, Lambert E. Walther, Otto F. Karbe, and Mrs. Sarah Spraggon. Photograph by Morris Schweig or Martin Schweig, 1914.

Charlotte Rumbold / 1869 – 1960

Charlotte Rumbold was park commissioner for the city. In 1914, she staged a large public pageant at Art Hill to mark the city's 150th anniversary. The pageant had a cast of more than 7,000. Over four days, more than 400,000 people saw the pageant. Including scenes about the Cahokia Indians and the Mound Builders, the pageant promoted messages to unite the city.

After the pageant, Rumbold demanded that city hall give her and her staff a raise. She was denied on the grounds she was not a voter. She was told that plenty of men would do her job for the same salary.

After moving to Cleveland, she spent the rest of her career doing social work.

Source: Valerie Schremp Hahn / St. Louis Post-Dispatch, July 3 – 9, 2020

Erma Bergmann / 1924 – 2015

Erma Bergmann, born in St. Louis, played softball and was recruited to play in a women's professional league. After she returned to home, she began a long career as one of the St. Louis police force's first commissioned policewomen.

Source: Valerie Schremp Hahn / St. Louis Post-Dispatch, July 3 – 9, 2020

Charlie Gitto Sr. / 1933 – 2020

Charlie Gitto Sr. and his wife, Annie, established several restaurants that helped shape the St. Louis dining scene. At one point, they operated six restaurants in the area along with their children.

In 1956, Gitto Sr. and Annie opened Gitto's Pizzeria on Macklind Avenue, their first restaurant. Their four children bussed tables and washed dishes at Gitto's Pizzeria before eventually owning their own restaurants. In 1978, the couple opened Charlie Gitto's Pasta House on Sixth Street downtown. It became a regular stop for visiting ballplayers and coaches with its proximity to the old Busch Stadium.

During the 1982 World Series, Charlie Gitto's Pasta House hosted eight major league managers at the same time. Gitto became friends with former Los Angeles Dodgers manager Tommy Lasorda. Lasorda, who ate breakfast with Gitto whenever he was in town, had his own table at the restaurant. Gitto Sr., a St. Louis restaurant icon, could be seen nearly every day sitting at the Gitto's Pasta House bar.

Source: Staff Reports / St. Louis Post-Dispatch, July 5, 2020

Luigi Amighetti / 1892 – 1956

Luigi Amighetti was an Italian immigrant who started a bakery on Daggett Avenue in 1917. Luigi's son, Louis, grew up working in the bakery. He traveled alone to Italy when he was 16 years old. Because of his Italian heritage, the authorities made him enlist into the Army. He escaped after two years and caught a ship ride back to the United States. He enlisted in the U.S. Army after Pearl Harbor and became one of the few to serve for both the Axis Powers and the Allies. While earning the rank of sergeant, he served as a cook.

After his service ended, he returned home to the bakery, which had moved in 1921 to Wilson Avenue across from St. Ambrose Catholic Church.

While he was living alone in an apartment above the bakery in 1965, two men threw a sheet over his head and beat him until he lost consciousness. The suspects were never found.

His part-time bookkeeper, Marge Sanders, became his second wife. In 1969, despite Louis's passion for baking, Marge decided that the bakery should begin selling sandwiches, called Amighetti Specials. In 1994, Marge and Louis sold the bakery.

The original bakery on the The Hill eventually shut down. The current owner, Anthony Favazza of the Favazza restaurant family, runs the Amighetti's restaurant on Manchester Road in Rock Hill and opened a new location on Southwest Avenue in the old Hanneke Hardware store. The construction manager of the new location was Chuck Shackelford, Louis's nephew and son of Gloria Amighetti. The architect is Ken Burns, the nephew of the owner of Hanneke Hardware store.

Source: Bill McClellan / *St. Louis Post-Dispatch*, July 4, 2020

Jerry Cox / Born 1925

Jerry Cox has been trailblazing innovative technologies in St. Louis for decades. In 1955, he came to St. Louis for a joint appointment at Central Institute for the Deaf and Washington University Medical School. In 1964, he founded the university's Biomedical Computer Laboratory, which later played a part in developing positron emission tomography (PET) scans.

In 1975, Cox created Washington University's computer science department. The department was one of the first to award doctorate degrees in the "new" discipline.

Later, he worked for Growth Networks, which was bought by Cisco Systems in 2000 for $355 million. He would go on to cofound Blendics, which created technology that enabled speedy design of computer chips.

Cox, still an emeritus professor at Washington University, started Q-Net Security in 2015. In 2020, the Olivette-based business landed a $3 million contract to develop its technology for the U.S. Air Force. The company is backed by a venture capital firm from Omaha, Nebraska, the National Innovation Fund. Q-Net developed a device, just barely bigger than a deck of cards, that monitors network traffic and blocks anything that isn't from an authorized source.

Known for finding solutions to big, complex problems, Cox has had a profound influence on computing, especially in the biomedical industry.

Source: David Nicklaus / *St. Louis Post-Dispatch*, July 17, 2020

Richard Henmi / 1924 – 2020

Richard Henmi was a Japanese American architect who excelled within the midcentury modern design movement. He was largely responsible for ushering in the megastructure style of living in St. Louis.

Henmi grew up in Fresno, California. In 1942, he was sent to a World War II internment camp at age 18. Later in 1942, he came to St. Louis to study architecture at Washington University. A number of U.S. colleges offered admission to Japanese students, which allowed them to leave the internment camps, but only Washington University offered slots in an architecture school. While in St. Louis, Henmi met and married Toyoko Hidekawa.

In 1945, Henmi enlisted in the Army and served for two years. Upon his return to St. Louis in 1947, he graduated from Washington University.

In 2003, Washington University's architectural school awarded Henmi with its Distinguished Alumni Award.

In St. Louis, he was known for creating the "Flying Saucer," a small building at Grand Boulevard & Forest Park Avenue in midtown. The building opened as a Phillips 66 gas station in 1967. The structure was part of the Council Plaza, also designed by Henmi, which was a mostly residential high-rise development financed by the Teamsters Union. The development is included in the National Register of Historic Places.

The station's roof, which is how the UFO-inspired nickname came to be, is actually a hyperbolic paraboloid supported by four posts and made of thin-shell concrete. The gas station became a Naugles in the mid-1970s. Then it was home to a Del Taco. In the early 2010s, preservationists saved the structure from being razed for a new development. Since 2012, the building has been a Starbucks and Chipotle.

The Mansion House Center, which is located along North Fourth Street in downtown St. Louis, is Henmi's most significant work. Built between 1964 and 1966, the Mansion House Center includes three residential towers and three

three-story office buildings. This project is credited with bringing high-rise apartment living to the St. Louis riverfront and also ushering St. Louis into the age of design concepts that include residential and commercial services in one large structure, called the "megastructure."

In the late 1950s, Henmi served as president of the local Japanese American Citizens League. In this role, he helped propose the 14-acre Japanese Garden at the Missouri Botanical Garden, which made its debut in 1977.

Henmi died in 2020 at a nursing home in Webster Groves.

Source: Joe Holleman / *St. Louis Post-Dispatch*, July 16, 2020

Random Bits

⚐ Native American mound builders lived in the St. Louis area as part of the Mississippian culture from the ninth century to the 15th century.

Source: *St. Louis Post-Dispatch*, March 15, 2020

Northeast view of St. Louis from Illinois shore, 1840, showing Big Mound. The view of St. Louis from the northeast by George Wooll was made after a lithograph by John Caspar Wilde from 1842 – 1844. Copyright Missouri Historical Society, St. Louis.

◀ Marine Drive near Creve Coeur Lake is named for a farmer, John Marine.

◀ Sinks Road in North County is named for a farmer, Powell Sinks.

◀ Wellston was named after a transportation pioneer, Erastus Wells.

◀ Champ was named after a developer, Norman B. Champ.

◀ Affton was named after a storekeeper and postmaster, Johann Aff.

◀ Walt Whitman's brother, civil engineer Thomas "Jeff" Whitman, was a St. Louis Water Commissioner. Walt came to visit his brother in 1879. He loved St. Louis but despised the "pungent gas" and "smut" that filled the air. There is a photograph from 1876, when cholera was still a plague, showing Jeff sitting at a biergarten. He was likely drinking beer because it was safer than water at the time.

Sources: Valerie Schremp Hahn / *St. Louis Post-Dispatch*, March 17, 2019; *St. Louis Magazine*, March 2018

Thomas Jefferson "Jeff" Whitman, Walt Whitman's brother, full-length portrait, seated, facing left. Photograph by Mathew B. Brady, circa 1888.

Walt Whitman, head-and-shoulders portrait, facing left. Photograph by Mathew B. Brady, circa 1888.

Hon. Erastus Wells, circa 1860 – 1875. Photograph from the Brady-Handy Collection of the Library of Congress Prints and Photographs Division.

RESTAURANTS

St. Louis has always been known as a foodie destination. From Tony Faust's Oyster House (a Faust married a Busch, and that couple purchased the estate that is now known as Faust Park in Chesterfield), to Tony's, our town has had a national reputation for our quality and diverse establishments. Ever wonder how toasted raviolis came about? Go to any restaurant on The Hill and ask. Want to try a slinger? Visit Courtesy Diner. My family has always enjoyed going out to dinner and trying new places. When there is some history to be learned in the process? Even better. For example, 21st Street Brewers Bar on Chouteau is in the basement of what used to be the Schnaider Brewery, one of St. Louis's first and largest breweries.

As you read about the following restaurants, my wish is that you have dined in at least one of them and now know a little more about what makes it special.

Tony's

Tony's opened as Tony's Spaghetti House in 1946. Under the leadership of Vince Bommarito Sr., Tony's became the top fine dining establishment in St. Louis, winning local and national accolades.

Vince Bommarito Sr. died in 2019 at the age of 88. Vince's son, James Bommarito, took the helm of both Tony's and the more casual Anthony's Bar. In 2020, Tony's announced that they will be moving from downtown to Clayton.

Source: *St. Louis Post-Dispatch*, April 2, 2019

Al's Café

For 103 years, Al's sat on the southeast corner of Dekalb & Victor Streets, just east of Soulard. Attracting factory workers, truck drivers, and police officers, the restaurant served breakfast, burgers, and beers. In its heyday of the 1940s to the 1960s, several of the regulars came from Hager Hinge Manufacturing Company, American Car (a railroad car maker), a packing house, and a paper bag factory. The workers would work around the clock and come in after their shifts. The Thursday daily special was chicken mudega.

It was originally called Frank Boyer's Tavern. In 1918, Austrian immigrants Henry and Rosa Dietz bought the bar from the Boyers. Rosa's son from her first marriage, Adolph Schalk, tended the bar at night after working at Mangelsdorf Seed Co. during the day. Schalk bought the bar from his parents in 1921 and renamed it Adolph Schalk Tavern. When describing how the bar managed to remain open after Prohibition in the 1920s, Ludmilla Schalk, Adolph's wife, explained, "Liquor came in the back door and went out the front door." Shortly after World War II began, the name Adolph was not very popular, so they changed it to Al's Café.

The Schalks sold the bar to their son-in-law, Adolph "Al" Beczkala Sr. in 1942. Beczkala Sr. had married the Schalks' daughter, Helen. Their son, Adolph Beczkala Jr., was the fourth-generation owner.

They received an award from former Mayor Francis Slay for being in business 100 years. Al's Café closed for good in 2020.

Source: Joe Holleman / *St. Louis Post-Dispatch,* February 27, 2020

A view of the commercial St. Louis riverfront and Eads Bridge. A sign for the Mangelsdorf Seed Company, 500 S. Main Street, is prominent in the photograph. 1930. Photograph from the St. Louis Riverfront Lantern Slides collection of the St. Louis Public Library.

Tompkins by the Rack House

According to local lore, the Rack House is a haunted restaurant. It is said that at least one ghost lives in the historic Mother-in-Law House on Main Street in St. Charles.

In the middle of the 19th century, Francis Kremer built the house and split it into halves for his family and mother-in-law. Supposedly, the mother-in-law's spirit now haunts the house. According to Troy Taylor, author of *The Big Book of Missouri Ghost Stories*, "Many customers have spoken of strange phenomena, including glasses, drinks, and utensils disappearing with no explanation, water glasses mysteriously spilling, coffee cups dumping their contents in the laps of guests, and food inexplicably changing temperature."

As of 2021, Tompkins by the Rack House is owned by Bridgette and John Hamilton.

Source: Ian Froeb / *St. Louis Post-Dispatch*, November 8, 2019

Bevo Mill

Bevo Mill, and its historic windmill, was built in 1916 by August A. Busch Sr. to serve as a rest stop on his way home from the Anheuser-Busch brewery to his estate at Grant's Farm. In 2017, the south St. Louis landmark was renovated and reopened as Das Bevo restaurant. It is now used for private events.

Source: Robert Cohen, *St. Louis Post-Dispatch*, November 17, 2019

Schneithorst's world-renowned Bevo Mill in St. Louis. The Bevo Mill, at 4749 Gravois Avenue, was erected in 1916 by August A. Busch. There are two painted scenes inside the entrance. This image is a Genuine Curteich-Chicago 'C. T. Photo-Colorit' postcard from 1934.

The Bevo Mill Restaurant at Gravois Avenue & Morgonford Road in St. Louis, photographed by John Margolies, 1988.

Old Barn Inn Restaurant

Built in 1843, the Old Barn Inn is located in St. Albans. It was originally built as an actual barn before being transformed in 1928. It currently offers farm-to-table service.

Source: *Chesterfield Lifestyle* magazine

Schneithorst's Restaurant & Bar

Schneithorst's Restaurant & Bar, located at 1600 South Lindbergh Boulevard, was built in 1956 by Arthur Schneithorst Jr. His father, Arthur Schneithorst Sr., operated Bevo Mill in the 1930s and 1940s, earning the family's reputation for good German fare. Younger generations kept the restaurant running since it opened.

Stan Musial was a lunchtime regular, and the spot also hosted events such as the St. Louis Blues Halloween party.

At one point, the restaurant comprised of 40,000 square feet, nine banquet rooms, and three dining rooms. But the business began to change in 2002. By 2005, the Hofamberg Inn, known for its sauerbrauten and wiener schnitzel, was gone. The Bierskellar bar and Kaffee Hause continued to undergo changes over the years. Jim Schneithorst Jr. announced the restaurant's closure in 2019.

Source: Bryce Gray / *St. Louis Post-Dispatch*, December 24, 2019

Failoni's

Failoni's opened in 1916 to serve cold drinks and hot lunches to workers at the steel mills, clay mines, and brick factories along Manchester Avenue. The restaurant was originally owned by Alex Failoni before his son, Alex Sr., ran the business for 60-plus years.

The original Alex was born in northern Italy before moving to Chicago at age 16 in 1901. He then worked at steel mills in Gary, Indiana. After that, he and a brother moved to St. Louis to work for Scullin Steel Co. The Scullin Steel Co. plant was located across the street from the bar, sprawled along the south side of Manchester Avenue. The bar, located at 6715 Manchester, was owned by Lemp Brewery at the time. Alex bought the business and building from the brewery.

Prohibition put a major dent in sales, so Alex sold bootleg alcohol and operated the restaurant as a speakeasy. Eventually the police started to crack down, and Alex had to cease operating that way. Alex decided to lease the building to a man who operated a soda-and-sandwich shop in 1925. He returned to work for Scullin until Prohibition ended in 1933 then took back the business.

In the background of this photograph, likely taken near the Southwest Avenue bridge, several factories are visible, including the Scullin Steel Co., located at 6700 Manchester. Photographed by Richard W. Lemen, June 16, 1926.

In 1950, Alex died unexpectedly. Alex Sr. was only 18 years old at the time, so Joe Failoni, his uncle, joined the business. Joe was a St. Louis policeman and one of the city's first motorcycle cops. He helped run the business until 1978, when he became director of Kiel Auditorium and the St. Louis Convention Center.

At that time, the bar was passed on to Alex Sr. Three generations of female family members — Rose, Rosemary, Rosetta, and Josie – have also helped run the place for the last 100 years. The restaurant was always closed at 10:00

p.m. during the week because the Failonis lived upstairs and raised their family there.

In 2016, the establishment celebrated its 100th anniversary. The restaurant is currently run by brothers Victor Failoni, and Alex Failoni Jr., and Alex's nephew, Joe Meiners.

Source: Joe Holleman / *St. Louis Post-Dispatch*, May 28, 2016

Queeny Tower

Queeny Tower at Barnes Hospital opened in 1965. The 18-story tower offered well-to-do patients manicures, pedicures, hair styling, and room service.

Barnes Hospital annual staff photograph. 1944. Photograph from the Becker Medical Library, Washington University School of Medicine.

It was the brainchild of Edgar M. Queeny, the founder of Monsanto Co. and the Barnes board chairman. He paid half of the $9 million construction cost. He wanted to be able to serve the patients from out of town who would come for laboratory tests that took days.

Nestled under a bronze-and-glass solarium roof on the 18th floor, there was a swimming pool. Below that was the full-service restaurant. Queeny Tower was very swanky, with original artwork, wood paneling, and plush carpeting. The restaurant had white tablecloths, an executive dining room, a small cocktail lounge, and floor-to-ceiling windows offering beautiful views into Forest Park and Steinberg Rink. The restaurant served its last sit-down meal in 2016 (it remains open for catering and for carry-out orders for employees). The pool area now houses heating, ventilation, and cooling equipment. The rest of the tower now serves as doctor's offices and the headquarters for the hospital's cardiac and vascular center.

Source: Joe Holleman / *St. Louis Post-Dispatch*, October 30, 2016

The Pat Connolly Tavern

In 1942, The Pat Connolly Tavern opened in the Dogtown neighborhood at the corner of Oakland & Tamm Avenues. There has been some confusion about the actual name of the bar. Shortly after it opened, a Griesedieck Bros. brewery wall sign was painted, labeling the bar "Pat's Tavern." Then, a Budweiser sign called the bar "Pat's Bar & Grill."

Tom McDermott, a main bartender in the 1940s and 1950s, bought the business in 1960. The Connollys maintained ownership of the building. At that point, the bar became "McDermott's." Then after that, Tom added a sign that said, "McDermott's Fine Foods."

In 1980, the Connollys bought the bar operation back. Paul Jovanovich, who married Pat Connolly's daughter Teresa, bought the business. Joe Jovanovich, a son of Paul and Teresa, is also a current owner. They changed the name of the bar to "Pat's."

Before buying the bar, Paul was a bartender at Walter Mitty's in Clayton in the 1970s. Teresa was a French teacher at

Mehlville and McCluer North high schools. The Connolly and Jovanovich families have lived in Dogtown since the 1920s.

Jack Buck was a regular customer, and Paul Newman dined there with executives from Anheuser-Busch. The establishment turned 75 in 2017, and they commissioned local artist Craig Downs to create a mural that flows along a retaining wall on the bar's east side. He also re-created the old Griesedieck mural on the building several years ago.

Source: Joe Holleman / *St. Louis Post-Dispatch*, January 22, 2017

Gus' Pretzels

In 1920, Frank Ramsperger baked pretzels in his basement in south St. Louis to support his family after an eye injury as a riveter. August Koebbe Sr. married Frank's daughter, Marcella, in 1944.

In 1952, August took over the bakery and named it Gus' Pretzel Shop. August and Marcella had seven children, all of whom spent time in high chairs and playpens at the back of the shop while their parents worked.

Gus Jr. bought the business from his dad in 1980. He remembers as a kid taking a basket of pretzels to sell to workmen for a nickel apiece on the new Interstate 55. Also that year, Gus Jr. married Suzanne, his college sweetheart. Gus Jr.'s brother David helped to run the business before that generation stepped back to allow Gus III, Gus and Suzanne's son, to take over.

The business at 1820 Arsenal Street that has been serving pretzels for over 100 years believes the stick shape is unique to St. Louis.

Source: *St. Louis Post-Dispatch*, January 10, 2020

SERVICES

I have lived in Kirkwood since 2011. When my wife and I were looking to move into a house with more space (with our second child on the way), we realized that we could not live far from a train station due to our four-year-old's love of trains. Getting to sit on Santa's lap inside the historic Kirkwood train station is a BIG deal for our son. Services that we take for granted, such as railroads, post offices, and airports, likely have a deep history and influence on the development of our area. Those three beautiful water towers standing in our city? Not many people realize that St. Louis was a leader in the purification of drinking water. And if it wasn't for Albert Bond Lambert's affinity for aviation, we may not have our international airport.

The following information will tell you more about the sometimes humble, nondescript, unglamorous services that played a big part in the development and growth of the city.

Chesterfield Postal Villages

Justus Post founded the town of Chesterfield in 1818. But until the St. Louis, Kansas City, and Colorado Railroad established a stop at Drew Station between Bonhomme Creek and Olive Street Road in 1887, there was no true town.

Also in 1887, Christian Burkhardt bought 21 acres between the railroad tracks and Olive Street Road. He built a general store next to Drew Station and sold other lots for businesses and homes. From 1895 until 1914, the Chesterfield Post Office occupied a corner of Burkhardt's store. In 1914, the post office moved across the street to the west side of the Farmer's State Bank building. Edward Burkhardt, Christian's son, served as the postmaster from 1895 to 1934.

In 1934, G. K. Spalding became postmaster and held that position until 1967. That year, the post office was relocated to 15755 Olive Boulevard. Francis Everett Konneman Sr. is known to be one of the first men to deliver mail on horseback from the Chesterfield Post Office. He delivered three letters on his first trip in 1895. Years later, Joe Schwenk delivered mail using a horse and buggy. By the 1920s, the automobile had replaced the horse and buggy.

The village of Monarch also developed next to a railroad stop. In the late 1870s, near the intersection of Centaur & Eatherton Roads was a stop for the Chicago, Rock Island, and Pacific rail line. William E. Sutton built his general store on the northwest corner of the intersection. The general store also served as a hotel, saloon, dwelling, and post office. The post office operated from 1895 until 1907, when the mail was transferred to Chesterfield. Sutton was the only postmaster to serve in Monarch.

The town of Loehr was founded by William Loehr in 1895. It was located at the intersection of Baxter & Clayton Roads. The residents called the area String Town. The town's businesses included Fred Merten's blacksmith shop, a general merchandise store owned by the Schrum family and later the Merten family, Joseph Feiner's stonemason business, Frank Eirten's saw and grist mill, and a post office, which was established in 1897. William Loehr served as postmaster until 1902. That year, the mail was transferred to St. Louis and then to Chesterfield.

In 1871, the community of Lake on Olive Street Road at Hog Hollow Road received its first post office. Lake was originally founded as Hog Hollow in the 1850s but was renamed in 1872. A mile marker was located in front of the post office, noting the distance of 18 miles from St. Louis. From 1880 until 1905, the post office was located in the Schaeper-Zierenberg General Merchandise store. The store also housed a hotel, blacksmith shop, icehouse, community center, and a service station. A one-room schoolhouse for the town was located nearby as well.

The postmasters included Charles H. Steinfeldt (1871 – 1872), Herman Schaeper (1880 – 1893), Anna W. Schaeper (1894 – 1897), and Ernst W. Zierenberg (1900 – 1905). Anna Schaeper was one of only four females in the area to hold a postmistress position. The others were Ann Hinze of Lake, Pearly B. Gray of Bellefontaine, and Frances Leiweke of Centaur. In 1905, the post office closed, and the mail was transferred to Bellefontaine.

Gumbo, the community located near Olive Street & Long Roads, received its first post office in 1882. The village was named for its rich, silty soil, which turned into gumbo mud when wet. During Henry Wetzel's time as postmaster, the post office was located in his store on the southeast corner of the intersection. In 1901, George Glaser became postmaster, and his home served as the post office. The village of Gumbo also contained a restaurant, hotel, blacksmith shop, doctor, and St. Thomas Evangelical & Reformed Church.

In 1891, the town of Centaur was founded by Anton Leiweke at the intersection of Olive Street & Eatherton

Roads. The town, situated on the Chicago, Rock Island, and Pacific Railroads, had a population of 50, a railroad station, general store, blacksmith shop, lime quarry, hotel, lumber mill, St. Anthony's Catholic Church, one-room schoolhouse, and stave factory. Leiweke also founded the Centaur Lime Company along with Jacob Theis, John Druhe, and Frank W. Holtschneider.

In 1891, Holtschneider became the first postmaster of Centaur. He served until 1900. From 1900 until 1959, four Leiwekes (Joseph, Leo, Otto, and Frances) served as postmaster. Postmasters traveled a 25-mile route by horse and buggy, which extended as far south as Fox Creek, west to Ossenfort Road, and east to Pond Road.

In 1907, the Chesterfield mail route included three free rural delivery routes and served about 2,000 people. The routes covered the villages of Lake, Bellefontaine, Chesterfield, Gumbo, Bonhomme, Orville, Monarch, and Loehr. In 1959, Centaur was added to the routes. The mail initially reached the area on a postal stagecoach before arriving by railroad. The mail was delivered in an orderly and timely manner despite the small population and large physical area. It was delivered in the rain, sleet, and dark of night. At first, residents collected their mail from the general store. In 1895, mail was being delivered on horseback. Horseback eventually was replaced with horse and buggy, which was then replaced by mail cars.

Source: Ann Chrissos / *Out & About*, January – March 2020; April – June 2020

St. Louis County Water Works

The first organized water system in St. Louis County began on the Missouri River at Hines Station in Chesterfield in 1902. This valuable service to St. Louis County residents offered a variety of employment opportunities and provided water service for more than 100 years. Women worked as typist clerks, file and mail clerks, and addressograph operators. Men worked as machine operators or in construction.

The St. Louis Water and Light Company hired John C. Walker from the Sedalia Water Company to help build the plant and to serve as the first superintendent. The foundation for the building that would house the pumps and steam boilers was laid out with stakes and string. Water pumped from the river through a 12-inch main for the first time in 1904. The main line, which ran from Hog Hollow Road to Denny Road (now Lindbergh Boulevard all the way to Kirkwood), served 3,000 customers. Walker also spearheaded the first stand tower built to store water. In 1908, the company laid a 12.8-mile cast-iron, 12-inch main from the plant to Kirkwood at a cost of $101,293.50.

Labor shortage was one of the biggest challenges during this time. Due to Chesterfield's small population, the company had to attract workers from St. Louis City. Commuting the 20 miles from the city was difficult because a horse and buggy was too slow, and there was only one train per day. The company then decided to build small homes across the street from the plant. At a cost of $8 per month, the workers could rent the homes, which included water and electricity.

Ott Biehle and Victor and Elmer Koester (nicknamed "Scrap"), Chesterfield residents in the 1930s, worked for the newly named St. Louis County Water Company.

The company was serving 33,000 customers by the time John C. Walker retired in 1931. His son, John E. Walker, began working for the water company at age 12. The company paid him $1 per day to pull weeds. He became a full-time employee after graduating from Ranken Trade School.

In 1931, the company converted from steam to electricity. Eventually, the company grew to serve 180,000 customers. The water plant used a generator from the 1904 St. Louis World's Fair. Some of the original buildings are still standing at the bottom of Hog Hollow Road.

In 2000, American Water Works acquired the St. Louis County Water Company. It is now operating as part of Missouri American Water.

Source: Ann Chrissos / *Out & About*, October – December, 2016

Grand Avenue, Bissell Street, Compton Hill Water Towers

At one time, there were roughly 500 standpipe water towers across the country. Now, there are seven remaining. St. Louis plays host to three of them. The historic towers each stand at least 150 feet tall, and each features a different type of architectural style. Not only did the towers help people locate their neighborhoods, during the late 1800s and early 1900s, they also kept the water system from exploding.

At this time, the city water system was piston-driven, so a large amount of water would be pushed out and return in surges. In 1912, the city water plant began using a spinning pump that produced a steady flow of water.

Completed in 1871, the Grand Avenue Water Tower at Grand & 20th Street is the oldest of the three towers. Made of brick and stone with cast-iron trim, it stands 154 feet tall. Several businesses in the area included "tower" into their names, including the Tower Theatre at Grand & West Florissant.

In 1885, the Bissell Street Water Tower at Bissell & Blair Avenues was erected. Designed to look like a Moorish minaret, the 206-foot tower is the tallest of the three. The Grand

Avenue and Bissell Street Water Towers were both built in North St. Louis because of the proximity to the Bissell Street water treatment plant.

General view from south of the Compton Hill Water Tower, Reservoir Park, Grand & Russell Boulevards & Lafayette Avenue, St. Louis. Photograph from the Historic American Buildings Survey collection of the Library of Congress Prints and Photographs Division.

In 1897, the Compton Hill Water Tower was built. Located next to the Compton Hill reservoir at South Grand & Russell Boulevards, it stands 179 feet tall. It was designed by Harvey Ellis, who also designed St. Louis City Hall. The water tower was in service until 1929. The water department used the tower to mount its dispatch antennas until 1984. Area residents formed a support group to spearhead a $19 million restoration of the Compton Hill Water Tower, completed in 1999. The tower is now open for tours.

The towers were a source of pride, as their presence meant people no longer needed to have a well or cistern to get water.

Source: Joe Holleman / *St. Louis Post-Dispatch*, July 10, 2016

The Bissell ("New Red") Water Tower was built in 1885 – 1886 from design plans by Deputy Building Commissioner William S. Eames, a founder of the St. Louis chapter of the American Institute of Architects and uncle to famous designer Charles Eames. It was completed at a cost of $79,798 and was in service until 1912. Constructed from red brick, light gray stone, and terra cotta, the tower stands 194 feet high and is located at Bissell Street & Blair Avenue in St. Louis. The interior of the tower once contained a spiral staircase that led to a balcony at the top, but that staircase has since been removed. Postcard published by the St. Louis News Co., Inc., St. Louis, circa 1910.

Lambert–St. Louis International Airport

Albert Bond Lambert is the namesake of Lambert–St. Louis International Airport. He was born in 1875. His father owned Lambert Pharmacal, which made Listerine. The family home was located on Vandeventer, where a young Albert staged musical and circus-style shows.

Four sailors with the *Spirit of St. Louis*, Col. Charles Lindbergh's famous plane, June 12, 1927. Photograph from the National Photo Company Collection.

In his 20s, he became an Olympic golfer. He competed in the 1900 Olympic Games in Paris and then at the 1904

World's Fair in St. Louis. The Olympic course in St. Louis, Glen Echo Golf Club, was owned by his father-in-law.

Aerial view of Lambert Field including terminals, hangars, runways, and aircraft (biplanes), postmarked 1944. Photograph from the St. Louis Public Library Digital Collections.

Albert began working for the family business, setting up factories in France and Germany. He became interested in hot-air balloons and learned to fly them while in Europe. Later, he was responsible for bringing a major balloon race to Forest Park. He trained balloon pilots for the U.S. Army and earned the rank of major. Lambert fell in love with airplanes, so he learned to fly with the Wright Brothers and earned his license.

In 1920, he leased the Bridgeton farmland that eventually became the airport. Lambert cleared the land and graded it into an airfield using his own money. He also built a hangar that any aviator could use for free. Albert played a huge part in bringing the 1923 International Air Races to St. Louis. The event drew around 200,000 spectators. In his honor, the airfield was christened Lambert St. Louis Flying Field.

Charles Lindbergh flew to St. Louis to attend the races and decided to stay as an instructor. Albert became one of Lindbergh's first financial supporters, along with other wealthy St. Louisans, for the trans-Atlantic flight. Lindbergh named his plane *Spirit of St. Louis.*

After the lease expired, Lambert bought the property. In 1928, Albert sold his 170-acre flying field in northwestern St. Louis County, plus an option on an adjoining 76 acres, to the city of St. Louis for $60,000, which was half the market value. The 246 acres eventually became the current airport.

From 1930 to 1970, the airport was called Lambert St. Louis Municipal Airport. Some people floated the idea to remove "Lambert" from the name. More than 200 people wrote letters opposing the change, and 5,000 people signed a petition. Charles Lindbergh was also publicly against removing "Lambert" from the airport name. In 1971, the name changed to Lambert–St. Louis International Airport.

Overhead photograph of St. Louis's Lambert Field showing terminals and runways on a natural-color postcard made in Milwaukee by the E. C. Kropp Co. and published by the St. Louis Greeting Card Co., postmarked 1943, circa 1940.

Lambert's residence was in the upscale Hortense Place in the Central West End. He was a dedicated fisherman, motorcyclist, and member of the Board of Police Commissioners. He tried to crack down on gamblers and reckless motorists.

"Aviation history, and the history of St. Louis, would have been much different but for the vision of Albert Bond Lambert," wrote Daniel L. Rust in his 2016 book *The Aerial Crossroads of America: St. Louis's Lambert Airport*. In 1933, Lambert Airport served 24,113 passengers. In 2019, the airport served 15.9 million passengers.

Sources: Leah Thorsen / *St. Louis Post-Dispatch*, August 21, 2016; *St. Louis Magazine*, July 2020

Kirkwood-Carondelet Rail Line

Constructed in the early 1870s at a cost of $300,000, the Kirkwood-Carondelet rail line routed freight around St. Louis City and delivered a U.S. president to his home in Grantwood Village. It spanned 14 miles and was built around the city of St. Louis to relieve rail congestion on the St. Louis riverfront. In addition to being a freight line, the Grant family and Busch family used it for passenger services.

Landowners were unhappy with the railroad using right-of-way easements for the new route. They were also not pleased with the property price purchases. To help out, the Grant family gave the Pacific Railroad an easement at no charge. President Grant would stop at the Kirkwood Train Station in transit from Washington, DC to his White Haven farm in South County. He had his own Pullman railroad car, which was gifted to him by William Vanderbilt. According to an 1873 copy of *The St. Louis Democrat*, the people in attendance to see Grant's arrival included Capt. John Dent, G. S. Greeley, Sen. Levi Morton, Dr. Edgar, Col. W. R. Holloway,

C. H. Ramsey, Judge John F. Long, and General A. G. Edwards. Also, Harry S. Truman stopped at the Kirkwood Train Station. According to some accounts, it was also used for Jefferson Barracks troop transports during World War II. Overtime, the rail line became unpopular with local residents due to freight trains blocking wagons and automobile traffic. By the 1950s, fewer manufacturers and shippers were utilizing the rail line. By the 1980s, the rail line was rarely used for any local rail traffic. By 1990, Missouri Pacific had halted service along the Kirkwood-Carondelet spur.

In 1991, Trailnet purchased the rail corridor. Despite heavy opposition from some property owners who wanted the land along the railroad ceded back to them, St. Louis County Parks and Recreation Department and Trailnet opened the first section of Grant's Trail in 1994. At the time, this section was known as the Carondelet Greenway Trail. Great Rivers Greenway eventually took over the trail's development, and by 2006, the total length was eight miles.

Hikers and bikers now call it "Grant's Trail," many not knowing that it used to be a railroad line. Now attracting 500,000 visitors per year with views of ponds, wetlands, and Gravois Creek, Grant's Trail has become a popular recreational attraction.

Source: Don Corrigan / *Webster-Kirkwood Times*, December 13 – 19, 2019

SPORTS

Is there anything more "St. Louis" than Cardinals baseball? Depending on when you were born, if you grew up playing baseball in St. Louis, you wanted to be Stan "the Man" Musial, Ozzie Smith, Mark McGwire, Albert Pujols, or Yadier Molina. Do you realize that Stan Musial played his entire career with the same organization? Not many athletes in any sport can claim that feat.

Following Mark McGwire as he chased Roger Maris's record of home runs in a single season was like nothing I have ever witnessed in sports. The ability of one man to bring an entire city together, rooting for the same goal, anxiously waiting for the next home run, getting lost in the excitement, was extremely special. The city was buzzing.

I crossed out something on my bucket list when I was fortunate enough to attend a Cardinals World Series game in 2013. My sister, who was born and raised in St. Louis but has lived in Minneapolis for most of her adult life, came back into town and surprised me with two tickets to a World Series game. The atmosphere was thick with edge-of-your-seat excitement. While we lost the game, being able to attend that game with her was something I will never forget.

While, like much of the town, I was crushed when the St. Louis Rams skipped town after the 2015 season, I am so lucky to have witnessed their 1999 Super Bowl run. I truly believe I was spoiled by that team, as that was my first football team. Not only was the atmosphere in the Dome deafening and electric, but the amount of talent on that team resulted in you attending games wondering not if the Rams were going to win, but how many points they were going to score. I was lucky that my dad had season tickets for those incredible years. Getting to see Kurt Warner, Torry Holt, Isaac Bruce, Marshall Faulk, Orlando Pace, and many more notable players was something I took for granted at the time. Most people remember "The Tackle," which resulted in the Rams winning the Super Bowl. But my favorite memory was "The Catch," when wide receiver Ricky Proehl made an incredible clutch catch in a playoff game in St. Louis versus Tampa Bay.

But St. Louis's sports legacy goes way farther back than my own life. Here are a couple quirky stories that are unique to St. Louis sports.

Ladies' Day Games

In the early 1900s, pretty much every ballpark across the country offered free or inexpensive admission to women on certain days. This concept was known as "the St. Louis idea." St. Louis Browns' president Robert Lee Hedges created Ladies' Day in 1912, offering free entry with a male escort. The Browns eventually decided to just let the ladies in after they realized that women were hanging around the ballpark trying to "sneak" their way in on any guy's arm. The St. Louis Cardinals followed suit.

By the 1930s, Ladies' Day games were packed with high school girls carrying textbooks, grandmothers, and mothers carrying their children trying to make their way through the crowd. They bought buttermilk, near beer, and ice cream with the money they saved on tickets. Despite not being popular with some male sports columnists, Ladies' Day would stick around for decades.

Source: Stefene Russell / *St. Louis Magazine*, April 2019

Elmer Brown, St. Louis American League, 1912. Photograph from the Bain News Service collection of the Library of Congress Prints and Photographs Division.

Satchel Paige

Satchel Paige was a Hall of Fame baseball player who spent the majority of his career playing in the Negro Leagues. But to Bill Purdy, a longtime St. Louis educator and school board member, he was the guy who hung out at his family's diner and called him "Billy."

Purdy spent 30 years working in St. Louis public schools, including several years as principal at Central and Roosevelt high schools. He retired in 1990 and was elected to the first of three terms on the St. Louis School Board.

Back in 1952 – 1953, Purdy was a batboy and bullpen catcher for the St. Louis Browns. As a 14-year-old, he won an essay contest about why you wanted to be a batboy. He took home $500 and spent the entire season as the team's batboy. He was rehired as a bullpen catcher in 1953. He was able to travel with the team and was included on team trips to movies and restaurants.

Purdy became close to Paige because Paige was a regular at Rex's Diner while playing for the St. Louis Browns. Purdy's father owned and operated the diner at North Newstead Avenue & Olive Street. Paige stayed at the Adams Hotel at Olive & Pendleton, which was one block east of the diner. When the Browns would return from road trips, Purdy's father would pick both of them up at Union Station and take Paige back to his hotel.

After the 1953 season, the Browns moved to Baltimore and Purdy lost touch with Paige. Purdy said about Paige, "One day in the locker room, he told me that no matter what I did when I grew up, I should be the best at it. He finished by saying, 'Billy, even if you end up being a waste hauler, then you be sure to haul more waste than anybody else.'"

Source: Joe Holleman / *St. Louis Post-Dispatch*, March 27, 2016

Random Bits

◁ The first professional baseball game in St. Louis was on May 4, 1875, and featured the St. Louis Red Stockings vs. the St. Louis Brown Stockings.

◁ Prior to becoming the St. Louis Cardinals in 1900, the team was known as the Brown Stockings, Browns, and the Perfectos. The Browns name returned in the early 20th century when St. Louis became a two-team city.

◁ Baseball manager/coaches born in the St. Louis area include Whitey Herzog, Yogi Berra, Red Schoendienst, Earl Weaver, and Dick Williams.

Source: Harry Levins / *St. Louis Post-Dispatch*, June 12, 2020

ODDS & ENDS

This might be the most fun section. A lot of people do not realize how many things St. Louis introduced to the world. One of the least important items, but still one I love having my out-of-town friends experience when they visit St. Louis, is the St. Paul Sandwich. Next time you are at a Chinese food restaurant, ask about it.

When I think about why St. Louis is responsible for so many "firsts," I remember that our city's nickname of "Gateway to the West" and our state's nickname of the "Show-Me State" both derive from our sense of building things, inventing things, creating things, and introducing things to the world.

I hope you enjoy reading these really weird, one-of-a-kind, random, and quirky facts that are unique to our area.

Missouri Leviathan

In 1840, a giant skeleton was unveiled at a dime museum on the St. Louis riverfront. According to a newspaper ad, the remains were of a beast that "made the earth tremble under the step of his feet." This beast was called the Missouri Leviathan, or the Missourium. The skeleton stood roughly 15 feet tall and 30 feet long. At one point, a three-piece band was hired to play inside its rib cage.

Albert C. Koch, the museum's owner who had a reputation by some as a carnival huckster, had discovered the bones himself. Koch, a German-born immigrant who was passionate about fossil collecting, dug up the skull near what is now Kimmswick, just south of St. Louis County. Initially thinking the remains were from a mastodon, he noticed that its right tusk stuck out sideways. Known for his flair for spectacle, Koch stated that this was a previously undiscovered animal that needed flared tusks to protect itself from floating debris as it was diving underwater for food. He eventually had enough to assemble a full display in St. Louis after finding more bones in the Ozarks.

In 1841, Koch sold the museum due to low ticket sales. He took the exhibit on a tour that ended in London. The superintendent of natural history at the British Museum, Richard Owen, determined that the Missouri Leviathan was in fact a composite of several mastodon specimens. Koch eventually agreed. Owen arranged for the museum to purchase the bones for the equivalent of roughly $153,000 today.

The area where Koch found the tusked skull is protected as Mastodon State Historic Site still today. You can still see the "Missouri Leviathan" at the Hintze Hall of London's Natural History Museum.

Source: *St. Louis Magazine*, May 2020

Missouri River Steamboats

In 1817, the *Zebulon Pike* arrived in St. Louis as the first Missouri River steamboat.

Steamboats traveling the lower Missouri River in the 19th century dealt with wrecks, disease, fire, explosions, crimes,

war, and ice. The Great St. Louis Fire of 1849 caused damage
to several before wreaking havoc on downtown. Steamboats
also contributed to the cholera epidemic in St. Louis that
killed 4,285 people.

The steamboats that operated on the Missouri River were
inexpensive to build and were not built to last. Three years
was the average life span of a Missouri River steamboat.
Mississippi River steamboats were built to last six years on
average.

The *Hermann* became the last steamboat to travel the
Missouri River when it ceased operation in 1935.

Source: Harry Levins / *St. Louis Post-Dispatch*, February 23, 2020

Great fire of 1849 from a lithograph, likely printed by Leopold Gast &
Brother. The St. Louis Fire of 1849 was a devastating fire that occurred
on May 17, 1849. This fire lasted over 11 hours, from 9:00 p.m. until 8:00
a.m. The paddle-wheeled steamboat *White Cloud* caught fire, escaped
its moorings, and drifted down the Mississippi River, spreading flames to
other steamboats, flatboats, and barges, then to buildings on the shore.
Everything on the waterfront level was on fire. Three lives, 430 buildings,
23 steamboats, nine flatboats, and several barges were lost from the fire.

The steamboat *City of St. Louis* cruises past the St. Louis riverfront. City buildings can be seen beyond the riverfront. Published by Frabicius Mercantile
Co., St. Louis, circa 1910.

Taken from a painting by Oscar E. Berninghaus for the collections of the
Boatmen's National Bank of St. Louis, the illustration shows the steamboat
J. M. White, which was known for its luxury, speed, and capacity. Photograph
from a lantern slide presentation for the 1964 bicentennial of St. Louis's
founding in 1764.

Sleeping Sickness of the 1930s

In 1933, Fred Green came to St. Louis County Hospital with
a fever and headache. He then slipped into a coma, and the

staff noticed his neck was stiff. He died a few days later. Other patients with the same symptoms began to show up. The sickness became known as St. Louis encephalitis. During the 1933 outbreak, 200 people died in St. Louis. During the three worst months of 1933, 1,000 cases were reported in the city and county combined. Some patients couldn't talk or keep track of time.

FOURTH VICTIM DIES
OF SLEEPING SICKNESS

Funeral Services For Mrs. C. Rodgers Held Sunday

Mrs. Cordelia Rodgers, 82 years old, of 103 West Cedar, who died last week, was the fourth Webster Groves victim to die of encephalitis.

Mrs. Rodgers, the widow of Dr. James W. Rodgers of Bowling Green, Mo., was buried in Bowling Green, Sunday afternoon. Rev. D. M. Skilling conducted the services in Webster Sunday morning.

Coming to Webster Groves in 1912, Mrs. Rodgers lived here almost continuously until her death. She is survived by two sisters, Mrs. A. G. Latimer and Miss Laura McMillin of 626 South Gore avenue, two daughters, Mrs. C. A. Prewitt of Los Angeles and Miss Claudine Rodgers of 103 West Cedar, and one son, James S. Rodgers of 45 S. Gore avenue.

Total of 24 Cases

According to Dr. C. C. Irick, city health commissioner, three deaths had previously been reported in Webster out of a total of 24 cases here. A total of 448 cases with 90 deaths was reported for St. Louis while the county had 488 cases and 78 deaths.

Records indicate that the epidemic has fallen off about 50 per cent in the county and 33 per cent in St. Louis. Several doctors predict that the epidemic will be over by the middle of October instead of the first of November, as was predicted some time earlier.

Cordelia Rodgers, "Fourth Victim Dies Of Sleeping Sickness," from the *Old Towne Crier*, September 28, 1933, courtesy of the Webster Groves Historical Society.

When federal and military experts came to St. Louis to investigate, they noticed the River des Peres, which served as a common sewer, smelled foul and had become a breeding ground for mosquitoes. The U.S. Public Health Service said you could dip a tumbler into the river and pull up a "living soup of larvae." We know now that the mosquitoes were the carriers of the disease.

An assistant professor of pathology in the Washington University School of Medicine, Dr. Margaret Gladys Smith, suggested a viral infection as the culprit. She went on to become a pioneer of pediatric pathology, and the medical school now gives high-achieving female students an award in her honor.

According to the Centers for Disease Control and Prevention, up to 20 Americans get infected each year. From 2009 to 2018, only six people across the country died from the disease.

Source: *St. Louis Magazine*, April 2020

Underground Railroad in Alton

Two local churches played critical roles in the underground operation. Organized in 1836, the Union Baptist Church in Alton is one of the oldest Black churches in Illinois. The newspaper pressman for abolitionist Elijah P. Lovejoy, John Anderson, started the congregation. Lovejoy was killed by a pro-slavery mob in 1837.

For slaves escaping Missouri as early as 1816, New Bethel-Rocky Fork AME Church in Godfrey was one of the first stops.

Source: Joe Holleman / *St. Louis Post-Dispatch*, February 17, 2020

Gooey Butter Cake

Johnny Hoffman worked for St. Louis Pastries Bakery, a baking cooperative. In the early 1940s, he created the cake by accidentally confusing the amounts of butter and flour. Restaurants in Milwaukee and Austin now serve their versions of gooey butter cake. Plain gooey butter cake can even be bought at Sugar Couture bakery in Brooklyn, New York.

Source: Joe Holleman / *St. Louis Post-Dispatch*, February 5, 2020

A Missourian Was President for One Day

David Rice Atchison, half-length portrait, facing three-quarters to left. Photographed by Mathew B. Brady, circa 1844 – 1860.

In 1849, the inauguration of Zachary Taylor as president landed on a Sunday. As a religious man, he refused to be sworn in on a holy day. According to some historians, the president pro tempore of the Senate and a Democrat from Missouri, Senator David Rice Atchison, served as U.S. president during those intervening hours. A plaque on his statue in Missouri declares him president for one day.

Source: *St. Louis Post-Dispatch*

Steam Rising from Sidewalk Cracks Downtown

Below the ground in downtown St. Louis lies the "steam loop," a network of pipes more than 15 miles long. These pipes carry pressurized steam throughout downtown. About 71 buildings get their heat from this network during the winter, many of which use the steam to heat water. These buildings include the Arch grounds, the Dome at America's Center, every city-owned building, the courthouses, and most big hotels. Busch

Stadium uses the steam to cook their hot dogs. The TUMS factory uses it to process their antacids.

The city of St. Louis owns all of the pipes. The steam itself is generated in a plant on the riverfront that is privately owned. The plant, just north of Laclede's Landing, is a Beaux-Arts brick-and-stone building erected by Union Electric in 1904. At the time, the plant generated both steam and electricity by burning coal. This electricity was responsible for lighting up the World's Fair.

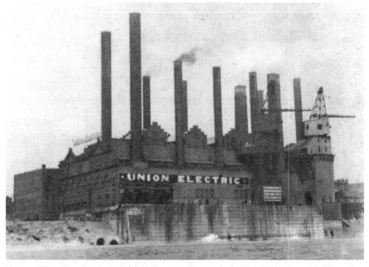

Union Electric plant at Ashley Street, St. Louis, 1930. Photograph from the St. Louis Riverfront Lantern Slides collection of the St. Louis Public Library.

Current owner Ashley Energy uses natural gas in what is called a cogeneration facility. The cogeneration facility burns natural gas to generate power then uses the waste heat to create steam. The steam is then tapped on its way out to make extra electricity. They claim that outside of solar or wind energy, their more than 80 percent efficiency is the best you can do.

With historic tax credits, many developers of loft buildings have found it more affordable to invest in their own boilers. This has caused usership to drop by roughly 45 percent in the past two decades.

Source: *St. Louis Magazine*, February 2020

A night view of the illuminated Palace of Electricity, Grand Basin, Louisiana Purchase Monument at the Louisiana Purchase Exposition (1904 World's Fair). The illuminated buildings at the Irish Village and the Tyrolean Alps concessions on the Pike and the sign for the Wabash Terminal can be seen in the distance. 1904. Photograph from the Louisiana Purchase Exposition Glass Plate Negatives collection of the St. Louis Public Library.

Golden Age of Automobiles in St. Louis

St. Louis played an important role in the development of the automobile industry. From the time of the Mississippian tribes to the present day, St. Louis has been a natural transportation hub, always embracing new modes of travel.

Dozens of car companies sprang up in St. Louis during the early part of the 20th century. By the 1950s, St. Louis was second only to Detroit in the volume of automobiles produced. Locust, Delmar, and Kingshighway were known as "Automobile Rows." The streets were lined with auto builders, dealers, repair shops, and tires and parts suppliers.

The former Carter Carburetor office is now the Grand Center Arts Academy.

Source: Jennifer Alexander / *Webster-Kirkwood Times*, December 6 – 12, 2019

Promotional photograph of a woman behind the wheel of a 1923 Dorris automobile. Photograph by John A. Conde from the St. Louis Auto Manufacturers Collection.

Iconic Cars Made in St. Louis

By 1965, St. Louis was producing more than 700,000 vehicles per year. The three Automobile Rows in St. Louis were lined with grand buildings where you could browse, test-drive, or repair vehicles. St. Louis was the home of the first gasoline station dedicated to serving motorists.

The Chevrolet Corvette, introduced in 1953 as America's sports car, was first mass-produced in St. Louis. The GMC CCKW truck, also called the "Jimmy," that carried supplies for Allied troops as they pushed eastward after the Normandy invasion during World War II, was built in St. Louis.

The Moon Motor Car Company, founded by carriage maker Joseph W. Moon, produced affordable, fully assembled mid-level cars with high-quality parts. Peaking with 10,271 vehicles sold in 1925, Moon Motor Car Company was in business from 1905 until 1930. The sleek Moon roadster that Walt Disney drove before selling it to finance the production of "Steamboat Willie" was a product of St. Louis.

Source: Jeannette Cooperman / *St. Louis Magazine*, December 2019

Image of a 1926 Moon Touring automobile, manufactured by the Moon Motor Car Company in St. Louis. Photograph by John A. Conde from the St. Louis Auto Manufacturers Collection.

A 1910 Moon Tourer, manufactured by the Moon Motor Car Company in St. Louis. Photograph by John A. Conde from the St. Louis Auto Manufacturers Collection.

Mississippi River

The Mississippi River was instrumental in slavery during the mid-1800s. In 1830, one in seven St. Louisans was an enslaved person.

The Missouri Leviathan, the bones of a beast believed to be an aquatic creature, was thought to have lived in the river.

Through the early 1900s, St. Louisans drank Mississippi water unfiltered. They could expect brown, opaque water to come out of their faucets. In the late 1800s, newspapers reported St. Louisans finding tiny worms and crabs in their water.

Source: Amanda Woytus / *St. Louis Magazine*, December 2019

Mississippi River at St. Louis. Steamboats wait their turn to be loaded or unloaded on the riverfront. Published by the St. Louis Post Card Co.

Eliza Hoole Marker in Tower Grove Park

Across the road from the West End picnic site in the southwest section of Tower Grove Park sits a stone marker. In 1882, the marker was installed in the park created out of Henry Shaw's personal land holdings.

Hoole was a cousin of Henry Shaw. In 1882, she came from England to visit and decided to plant an oak tree because she enjoyed her trip so much. Henry Shaw then had a marker installed with Hoole's name, the year, and the word "oak" on it. James Hoole, Eliza's father, was one of Henry Shaw's early investors. Eliza was very close with Henry Shaw, as his will and testament in 1889 set aside two hundred pounds sterling for her.

Henry Shaw House, 2345 Tower Grove Avenue, St. Louis. Photograph from the Historic American Buildings Survey collection of the Library of Congress Prints and Photographs Division.

Born in Sheffield in 1800, Henry Shaw emigrated to the United States and settled in St. Louis in 1819. He retired at 39, a successful hardware merchant and one of the largest landowners in the city. Later, he built Tower Grove House on his estate and funded and built what became the Missouri Botanical Garden on his land. The Garden opened to the public in 1859. He also donated the land adjoining his estate for Tower Grove Park to the City of St. Louis. Shaw died in 1889. Photograph from the St. Louis Bicentennial Celebration Lantern Slides collection of the St. Louis Public Library.

The tree eventually died or was removed. A local jogger has noticed that every November 1, a Halloween candle is left at the stone. It is unknown who leaves the candle.

Henry Shaw also installed a stone marker next to a mulberry tree in Flag Circle on Center Cross Drive. This marker honors Shakespearean actress Adelaide Neilson. She was a popular English actress who became famous in the U.S. In 1880, Neilson visited St. Louis and was so impressed with Shaw's statue of William Shakespeare that she told him she would send him a cutting from a mulberry tree at Stratford-upon-Avon, Shakespeare's hometown. But before Neilson could send the cutting, she died at the age of 33. So Shaw took it upon himself to import a cutting and plant it behind the statue. He then installed a marker honoring Neilson.

Source: Joe Holleman / *St. Louis Post-Dispatch*, December 4, 2016

Adelaide Neilson / J. Gurney & Son, Publisher, 5th Ave. cor. 16th St. New York. February 1874.

Victoria Water Lilies at the Missouri Botanical Garden

In the early 1800s, European botanists began noting the giant Victoria water lilies in South America. The Victoria water lilies are part of the aquatic Nymphaeaceae family. Seeds and specimens quickly found their way across the Atlantic. In 1852, gardener James Gurney grew the lilies in London at the Royal Botanic Gardens at Kew. At the time, a young Queen Victoria was enamored by the plants, and her name has been attached to them since.

Gurney eventually found a job with a wealthy Henry Shaw in St. Louis. Shaw was planning a large municipal garden. Over several years, Gurney worked his way up to be the head gardener at Shaw's Garden. In 1895, the Victorias he grew at Shaw's Garden helped attract more than 30,000 people one Sunday.

The pads of the *Victoria amazonica* specimens, native to the backwaters of the Amazon, reportedly grow up to 10 feet across, the largest in the wild. Their weakness is that they dislike cold water, so the hard summer rain in St. Louis can stall growth. The *Victoria cruziana* specimen is native to Bolivia and Argentina and is better at tolerating cold water. The pads of this specimen can grow up to 93 inches across. The pads of the Longwood hybrid specimen can grow up to 91 inches across, the record diameter being achieved at the Missouri Botanical Garden.

Source: *St. Louis Magazine*, March 2020

A view of the Palm House, gardens, and lily pond at the Missouri Botanical Garden in St. Louis. On opposite side: "Beacon series, made in U.S.A." Circa 1915.

A view from the Flora Avenue entrance across the lily pond to the Palm House at the Missouri Botanical Garden in St. Louis. In 1913 the Garden constructed the Palm House as a large greenhouse for tropical plants. The Palm House was demolished in 1959 and the Climatron built on its site. On opposite side: "Made in U.S.A. by E. C. Kropp Co., Milwaukee, WI." Circa 1940.

St. Louis Drinking Water

The most important civic improvement of the Progressive Era was St. Louis's great water purification. In the late 1800s, St. Louis tap water was brown and sludgy with river silt. The city made up for its awful water with "inexhaustible quantities of the best beer in the world," according to Walt Whitman.

In 1902, St. Louisan David Francis was planning the World's Fair. He met with St. Louis Mayor Rolla Wells with a sense of urgency because he was dead set on having clean water for the cascades at the summit of Art Hill. Wells promised to have clean water by the time the Fair opened in 1904, but when Francis pressed him on how, Wells replied, "I will not tell you how, Dave. Just take my word for it. I have a plan."

Politician Rolla Wells (1856 – 1944), who served two terms as mayor of St. Louis. Source: Flickr Commons project, 2010. Circa 1910 – 1915.

Feathery fountains above the Basin, Electricity, and Varied Industries Buildings, 1904. Photograph originally published by Underwood & Underwood.

The Four Great Fountains, Grand Basin, and the West Cascades from the Palace of Education roof, 1904. Photograph originally published the Keystone View Company.

Three months before the Fair, the water was still dirty. A brilliant chemist who worked for the city water department, John Wixford, came up with the Wixford Process. This process used incredible quantities of milk of lime to quickly rid the river water of sediment. On March 22, five weeks ahead of the Fair opening, fresh water flowed for the first time. Twenty million fairgoers enjoyed the sunlit, sparkling-clear fountains. Ninety thousand gallons of water per minute rushed down three terraced cascades to four fountains in the grand basin on the first day of the 1904 World's Fair.

There was a $10,000 competition to solve the dirty water problem, but because Wixford was an employee of the water department, he could not collect the prize. Possibly because Wells was scared the city would have to pay Wixford royalties on his forthcoming patent, Wixford was shut out of credit too. Wells also had backed an earlier, much more expensive solution, so the eccentric Wixford was easily cast aside.

Wixford lived his entire life on North Ninth Street in a three-story house with no running water. He used his first floor as his lab, and he opened the second floor to boarders who had nowhere else to stay. He slept alone on the third floor. "Clean Water Wixford" was known to do his own dental work with copper wire and frequently forgot to cash his paychecks. He rode a bike because he thought motorcars were too fast.

Source: *St. Louis Magazine*, February 2019

Jimmy Joe

Jimmy Joe was a purebred Clydesdale who spent 17 years as the carriage horse at Tower Grove Park. He came from an Amish community in Wisconsin that is known for breeding draft horses. He was known to pull just-married couples around the Victorian park in South St. Louis and sometimes offered his head and snout to be petted by visiting schoolchildren. Jimmy Joe has given about 2,700 rides. In 2016, he retired as a carriage horse to spend his time as a companion horse on a seven-acre estate in Wildwood.

Source: Joe Holleman / *St. Louis Post-Dispatch*, October 9, 2016

1904 Summer Olympics Marathon

A historical marker for the 1904 Olympic marathon is located in University City. The roughly four-foot-tall and five-foot-wide sign is on North & South Road, south of Shaftesbury Avenue. The sign reads, "Historical marker: Olympic marathon route of 1904."

It is unknown who erected the sign or who is responsible for it. University City and St. Louis County have both said the

sign doesn't belong to them. The land the sign sits on is owned by the Metropolitan St. Louis Sewer District, but they know nothing of who is responsible for maintenance of the sign.

According to news stories, the marathon occurred on August 30, 1904, with temperatures in the 90s and humidity at typical St. Louis levels. Thirty-one runners lined up to start and only 14 finished. The race itself was estimated to be between 23 and 25 miles, shorter than the 26.2-mile

Thomas J. Hicks. Winner of Marathon Race. The Olympic games, 1904. Photograph by Charles J. P. Lucas, circa 1904.

standard. The winner was an Englishman running for the United States, Thomas J. Hicks. It was said he kept going by drinking shots of French brandy, bits of strychnine, and warm water from a car radiator.

Start of Marathon Race. The Olympic games, 1904. Photograph by Charles J. P. Lucas, circa 1904.

After about nine miles, Fred Lorz of New York ceased running due to cramps. He caught a ride with a passing auto back to Francis Field, where he jumped out and ran to the finish line. The crowd cheered, the band blared, and Alice Roosevelt moved forward with a victory wreath. But angry race officials realized what Lorz had done and abruptly stopped the celebration.

John Furla, a St. Louisan who sold fruit at the World's Fair, raced for both his native country of Greece and his adopted hometown. He would eventually own St. Louis's largest fruit wholesale company in town before selling it in the 1930s.

Lentauw and Yamasini, two South Africans, came to the fair to work as concessionaires. Despite never running a marathon, both participated and finished the race.

The number four finisher and a crowd favorite was Felix Carvajal, a wiry Cuban postman. Known for running laps in the Havana city square before mounting a soapbox to plead for travel money to St. Louis, Carvajal was just barely over five feet tall. He made it to St. Louis wearing street shoes and long pants. Before the start of the race, he cut his pants into shorts. He was often seen chatting with spectators during the race.

Source: Joe Holleman / *St. Louis Post-Dispatch*, May 15, 2016

The David R. Francis Field, Washington University, St. Louis. The ornamental wrought-iron gate on the east end of the field was built after the World's Fair to commemorate the 1904 Olympics. During both the 1984 and 1996 Olympic Torch relays, the Olympic Flame passed by Francis Field on its way to the site of the Games. On verso: Postmark 1915.

Marathon Race. The Olympic games, 1904. Photograph by Charles J. P. Lucas, circa 1904.

Nation's First Interstate Highway

On August 13, 1956, a stretch of Interstate 70 in St. Charles County became the first interstate to begin construction after President Dwight Eisenhower signed the Federal Aid Highway Act.

Source: *St. Louis Post-Dispatch*, June 24, 2018

First American Viticultural Area (AVA)

The Augusta AVA, a 15-square-mile area around Augusta, became the first grape-growing region designated by the federal government. The Augusta AVA, first settled by German immigrants in the mid-1800s, gained its status in June 1980, eight months before the Napa Valley AVA in California.

Source: *St. Louis Post-Dispatch*, June 24, 2018

Interior of wine cellar at the Mount Pleasant Wine Company Buildings in Augusta, St. Charles County. Photograph from the Historic American Buildings Survey collection of the Library of Congress Prints and Photographs Division.

First President to Fly in an Airplane

In 1910, Theodore Roosevelt became the first president to take a ride in an airplane from Kinloch Aviation Field, in an area now known as Berkeley. The ex-president, visiting to attend the first international air show, reluctantly took a three-minute ride in a Wright brothers biplane. Before the show, he telegraphed the organizers: "Will visit the field, but under no circumstances will I make a flight."

Source: *St. Louis Post-Dispatch*, June 24, 2018

President Theodore Roosevelt and aviator Archibald Hoxsey in St. Louis. Photograph by Bain News Service.

World's First Steel Truss Bridge

The Eads Bridge, completed in 1874, is the world's first steel truss bridge and considered an engineering marvel. Considered a self-educated engineer, James Eads had built several ironclad gunships for the federal government but had never built a bridge before. According to the city of St. Louis, the bridge crossing the Mississippi River was the first to carry railroad tracks, the first to use tubular cord members, and the first to depend entirely on cantilever construction for its superstructure.

Source: *St. Louis Post-Dispatch*, June 24, 2018

Eads Bridge, St. Louis, circa 1903. Photograph from the Library of Congress Prints and Photographs Division.

American engineer James Buchanan Eads is best known for the triple-arch steel Eads Bridge over the Mississippi connecting St. Louis and East St. Louis, IL, which opened on July 4, 1874. His earlier endeavors included a salvaging business in St. Louis recovering cargo from riverboat disasters and manufacturing of ironclad steam-powered warships for the Union during the Civil War. A later project provided a year-round open navigation channel for New Orleans by means of jetties. Photograph originally published by Williams & Cornwell, circa 1870.

Onlookers standing north of the Eads Bridge survey the Mississippi River. Streetcars cross the Eads Bridge on the St. Louis riverfront. Photograph by H. H. Bregstone.

First School in the Western Hemisphere to Use Braille

A Frenchman named Louise Braille developed and perfected a system of "night writing" used by soldiers in the French army to communicate without using light that might attract attention from the enemy.

In 1851, the Missouri School for the Blind was founded in St. Louis. At the time, there were only about a dozen such schools across the country.

Around 1860, the Missouri School for the Blind adopted the English version, which became known as "Missouri Braille." Many of the first braille devices, such as slates and methods used to outline maps and figures, were developed by teachers and educators at the school.

Source: *St. Louis Post-Dispatch*, June 24, 2018

The Blind Girls' Home was established in 1867 by five women who had recently graduated from the Missouri School for the Blind. In 1886, the Home secured the use of the old Nicholson home at 1214 N. Garrison Avenue in North St. Louis. The Home remained in that location until 1909, when it was able to move into new quarters at 5235 Page Boulevard. Image by the Adolph Selige Publishing Co., St. Louis, circa 1910.

First Cocktail Party

According to the Missouri Historical Society, wealthy St. Louisans Julius and Sarah Walsh hired a bartender to mix a variety of drinks for their friends who came to their midday party. The party, in 1917, occurred at a mansion on Lindell Boulevard. At the time, the Walshes lived across the street at 4499 Lindell and didn't move into the site of the party until two years later. The site of the party, at 4510 Lindell, is now the present-day residence of the archbishop of the Archdiocese of St. Louis. After this party, more people in St. Louis and other cities hosted their own cocktail gatherings, until Prohibition. The cocktail party eventually became an American cultural phenomenon.

Source: *St. Louis Post-Dispatch*, June 24, 2018

St. Louis Police Department exhibit in the Palace of Education and Social Economy at the Louisiana Purchase Exposition (the 1904 World's Fair). A model jail, designed by the Pauly Jail Building Company, was part of the exhibit. Photograph dated 1904, photographer unknown.

First Police Department in U.S. to Use Fingerprints

In 1904, the St. Louis Police Department became the first department to use fingerprinting to identify criminals. The department learned the technique from a Scotland Yard official who came here to guard the crown jewels at the World's Fair.

The department also claims to be the first to adopt eight-hour shifts, in 1854. It is believed they were also the first department to organize a national police convention, held in St. Louis in 1871.

Source: *St. Louis Post-Dispatch*, June 24, 2018

The chief of the mounted police (right) stands with an unidentified man at a Louisiana Purchase Exposition building. The St. Louis Police Department, along with the Jefferson Guard, provided security services at the Louisiana Purchase Exposition (the 1904 World's Fair). The mounted police also accompanied exposition officials and dignitaries at parades and on other ceremonial occasions. Photograph dated 1903, photographer unknown.

First Drive-up Window

In 1930, the Grand National Bank became the first bank in the country to use the drive-up window for customers. The bank occupied the main floor and mezzanine of the Continental Life Building at Olive Street & North Grand Boulevard.

In the early 2000s, the building was renovated into apartments, but the old bricked-up window is still visible in the alley.

Source: *St. Louis Post-Dispatch*, June 24, 2018

Details at the top of the art deco Continental Life Building, located at Grand & Olive in St. Louis. The building was designed by architect William B. Ittner and was completed in 1930. Photograph circa 1935. Photograph from the St. Louis Lantern Slides collection of the St. Louis Public Library.

Tenth looking south at Olive. Left: Swope Shoe Company; right: Continental Life Insurance Building, Metropolitan Cigar Store, and Rens Cafeteria. Photograph by Richard W. Lemen, circa 1930.

First Monster Truck
In the mid-1970s, St. Louisan Bob Chandler modified a 1974 Ford F-250 pickup truck with 48-inch-tall tires. The "monster truck" appeared in the public for the first time in 1979. The first recorded monster truck crash occurred in 1981 as the truck, known as Bigfoot #1, crushed two cars in a field outside St. Louis.

Source: *St. Louis Post-Dispatch*, June 24, 2018

First Society of St. Vincent de Paul in the U.S.
In 1845 at the Old Cathedral, the first meeting of the Society of St. Vincent de Paul in the United States was held. A plaque was placed at the cathedral in 1945 to commemorate the 100th anniversary of the first meeting.

The society was founded in Paris 12 years earlier by a group of friends who wanted to help the poor. The Rev. Ambrose Heim, known as the "Priest of the Poor," was the spiritual adviser for the first group in St. Louis. He is buried in Calvary Cemetery.

Source: *St. Louis Post-Dispatch*, June 24, 2018

Entrance of the Old Cathedral, St. Louis. The Old Cathedral was built between 1831 and 1834 and named, like the city, for King Louis IX of France. Engraved in gold over the entrance to the church are the words, *In honorem s. Ludovici. Deo uni et trino dicatum.* A. MDCCCXXXIV, which translates as "In honor of St. Louis. Dedicated to the one and triune God. A.D. 1834." The word "Yahweh" also is inscribed in Hebrew above the engraving on the main entrance. From lantern slide presentation for the bicentennial of St. Louis's founding in 1764. Photograph dated 1964.

First Olympics in the U.S.

The first Olympics in the United States was hosted by St. Louis in 1904. Previously, the Olympic Games were held in Athens and Paris. The St. Louis Olympics was also responsible for introducing the gold, silver, and bronze medals. Also, runner George Coleman Poage became the first African American Olympic athlete to win a medal in the Games during the St. Louis Olympics. He won a bronze medal in the 200- and 400-yard hurdles.

Source: *St. Louis Post-Dispatch*, June 24, 2018

The Olympic games, photograhed by Charles J. P. Lucas in 1904.

First Kindergarten

After traveling to Germany and seeing the studies in form and color through play in Friedrich Froebel's classroom, Susan Blow had an idea. In 1873, she opened the first kindergarten along Michigan Avenue in Carondelet. Her Des Peres Elementary School classroom initially held 42 students. Nearly 8,000 children were enrolled in St. Louis kindergarten just seven years later.

Source: *St. Louis Post-Dispatch*, June 24, 2018

Susan Blow (1843 – 1916), American educator, was born in Carondelet. She opened the first public-school Kindergarten in the United States in the Des Peres School in St. Louis in 1873. In 1874, Blow opened a training school to prepare kindergarten teachers. The image of Blow with kindergarten students in the Des Peres School is from a mural by Gari Melchers in the Missouri State Capitol, Jefferson City.

France's First Grizzly Bear Came from St. Louis

Marie-Joseph Paul Yves Roch Gilbert du Motier, also known as the Marquis de Lafayette, was born into the French aristocracy. Wanting to be a part of the revolutionary cause, he sailed to America at age 19 and fought alongside American soldiers as one of the Continental Army's major generals. Some credit his father-and-son-like relationship with George Washington as a reason America won the Revolution. His legendary bravery is now highlighted in the Broadway show *Hamilton*.

After Lafayette finished his service in America, he sailed home to fight in the French Revolution. In 1825, he decided to revisit the sites of his American military campaigns and eventually made his way back to St. Louis after docking at Carondelet. Nearly all of St. Louis waited at the wharf for his arrival, and onlookers cheered as he came into sight. Lafayette was picked up in a horse-drawn carriage and taken to the home of Pierre Chouteau.

Before a fancy ball and supper at the Mansion House Hotel later that evening, Lafayette wanted to tour the nearby Indian mounds and visit with explorer William Clark. Clark, as superintendent of Indian affairs, had his own small museum of Native American artifacts, including four necklaces of large pale-to-dark-brown claws. Two decades earlier, Clark had first recorded grizzly bears on his journey west. Lafayette, noting that the London Cabinet of Natural History had only a single claw from America's most ferocious beast, was in awe. As a parting gift, Clark gave Lafayette a heavy buffalo-skin robe cut into a Russian riding coat. Lafayette gave Clark a mahogany mess chest, full of sterling, crystal, and bone china that he carried through the war.

After visiting Kaskaskia and Vandalia in Illinois, Lafayette returned to France where a baby grizzly bear had arrived as another gift. After being advised against keeping the bear as a pet, he donated the cub to the Jardin des Plantes in Paris, a 60-acre botanical garden and menagerie. As the bear neared 1,400 pounds, Lafayette dryly wrote to Clark, "His large vile and ferocious temper have since been developed."

Source: *St. Louis Post-Dispatch*, November 2018

The Suffragette Who Cast the First Vote by a Woman in Tennessee

Elizabeth Avery Meriwether, who cast the first vote by a woman in Tennessee, was once a resident of Grand Center.

Source: Colleen Schrappen /*St. Louis Post-Dispatch*, November 17, 2019

The Battle of St. Louis

In 1780, British and American forces fought near a 40-foot tower known as Fort San Carlos. The fort was located at the corner of Walnut & Fourth Streets, near where the Gateway Arch grounds are now. The roughly 700 residents of the small fur-trading town had heard for months that the British were planning an attack to gain control of the Mississippi River. According to traders traveling downriver, the British had roughly 1,000 soldiers and were stockpiling about 100 canoes for an attack. The British wanted to conquer both St. Louis and Cahokia. In addition to clearing the Americans from the Mississippi, they also wanted to take all of the livestock from St. Louis, Cahokia, Ste. Genevieve, and Kaskaskia. Knowing what was coming, the village built the fort and dug a trench that ran from present-day Laclede's Landing to Second & Lombard streets near Soulard.

In May, 700 British and Indian troops attacked from the north and northwest and ran into a trench occupied by about 300 American militiamen and 30 Spanish army members.

The American and Spanish fighters were under the command of Fernando de Leyba, the lieutenant governor and military commander in St. Louis. After a two-hour fight, de Leyba reported he lost 21 defenders, while the British had few casualties. But the British were not able to take over control of St. Louis. American militiamen under the command of Gen. George Rogers Clark were victorious over the 300 British soldiers on the Illinois side.

Left: Illustration of a French colonial-style residence common in early St. Louis. Right: Fort San Carlos built circa 1780 to defend the town of St. Louis against the British and Indian forces. Circa 1800s. Photographs from the Louisiana Purchase Exposition Glass Plate Negatives collection of the St. Louis Public Library.

The day before the attack, most of the town was celebrating the Feast of Corpus Christi in a common field. Because of this, the Indian scouts could not get close enough to the town to see the defensive situation. This could explain why the British went through with attacking such a fortified position in St. Louis.

This Battle of St. Louis prevented Great Britain from gaining control of the Mississippi Valley, which would have changed America as we know it. It is considered the western-most battle of the American Revolution. A marker was placed just outside the patio of the Hilton St. Louis at the Ballpark in 1946 by the General Society Sons of the Revolution. The marker's location is roughly a block west of the fort's location.

Sources: Joe Holleman / *St. Louis Post-Dispatch*, April 9, 2017; Valerie Schremp Hahn / *St. Louis Post-Dispatch*, April 3 – 9, 2020

Sketch of the fort erected in 1792 by Zenon Trudeau, lieutenant governor of the Spanish territory of Upper Louisiana. The earlier tower of Fort San Carlos is seen in the drawing. The site is at present-day 4th & Walnut Streets. Illustration from the St. Louis Lantern Slides collection of the St. Louis Public Library, circa 1900.

The Only Quaker Church in the St. Louis Area

A quaint brick building in LaSalle Park.

Source: Colleen Schrappen / *St. Louis Post-Dispatch*, November 17, 2019

A Chinese Royal Visited the World's Fair

Prince Pu Lun, at one time a contender for the Chinese throne, became the third member of the Chinese royal family to visit the United States when he came to St. Louis for the 1904 World's Fair. Breaking China's long isolation from the West, the 29-year-old prince came as an emissary to display the Fair's Chinese Pavilion. The pavilion, a replica of Pu Lun's country home, was the first grand-scale replica of traditional Chinese culture to the rest of the world. It included a pagoda of carved wood, ebony and ivory, silks, jades, dragons, gilded lions, scrolls, porcelain, and coins. A 17-foot portrait of the empress dowager, which sat inside the pavilion, is now in the Smithsonian.

At the Washington Hotel with a large posse with him, Pu Lun listened to American music and gave out roughly $1,000 in tips. He tried American cooking and acquired a taste for beef, potatoes, and hard-boiled eggs. A horse-drawn carriage was presented to Pu Lun by Adolphus Busch. According to newspapers, Pu Lun slept late into the morning, loved ice cream, and placed several wagers at the racetrack. He fell in love with American culture, which was important since his visit was a message to President Theodore Roosevelt.

Diplomacy eventually failed as U.S. immigration officials arrested many of the workers, merchants, and actors headed for the Fair. China then boycotted American goods in retaliation.

By 1912, China was a republic. Pu Lun never became emperor. Several of the pavilion's treasures were sold to pay for the passage home, winding up in private homes in St. Louis.

Source: *St. Louis Magazine*, January 2020

The Chinese prince, Pu Lun, a guest of Commissioner-General Theodor Lewald, with his party and Louisiana Purchase Exposition officials entering the Tyrolean Alps concession at the Louisiana Purchase Exposition (the 1904 World's Fair). From the Official Photographic Co., circa 1904 – 1905.

Model of entrance for China's pavilion for the 1904 World's Fair. A man and a boy unveil the model of the entrance to the China National Pavilion for the Louisiana Purchase Exposition as the building is erected behind them. The building reproduced the summer palace of Prince Pu Lun. Photograph from the Louisiana Purchase Exposition Glass Plate Negatives collection of the St. Louis Public Library, dated January 7, 1904.

China's pavilion for the 1904 World's Fair. Spectators view men at work at the China National Pavilion for the Louisiana Purchase Exposition. The Chinese Pavilion included three buildings and a garden. Architects Atkinson & Dallas of Shanghai designed the compound. Photograph from the Louisiana Purchase Exposition Glass Plate Negatives collection of the St. Louis Public Library, dated March 4, 1904.

The Chinese Pavilion's large pagoda, Louisiana Purchase Exposition, St. Louis, photograph from the Library of Congress Prints and Photographs Division, circa 1904.

Prohibition in St. Louis

On January 16, 1919, the Prohibition amendment was passed. The bartenders had shut off the remaining taps by January 17, 1920, the official start of constitutional Prohibition. The law intended to enforce the 18th Amendment, the federal Volstead Act, which made it illegal to even carry a pocket flask outside one's home. The Volstead Act allowed the sale of alcohol as prescription medicine only. The proprietor of a rooming house on South 10th Street, John Goheen, was caught on the sidewalk carrying two suitcases full of whiskey bottles.

For local gangs like Egan's Rats, Hogan's, and the Cuckoos, Prohibition was lucrative. After graduating from safecracking and banditry, they battled to satisfy the public's craving for alcohol and littered the streets with one another's bodies in the process. In 1925, St. Louis officers apprehended

179 suspected moonshiners. Jennie Buttee of 5115 Daggett Avenue was one of the suspects. She told officers she had no idea how a vat of 5,000 gallons of mash got into her basement. In 1930, agents raided a fashionable home at 3733 Pine Street, where 250 gallons were produced per day.

In 1922, the Chase Hotel at Kingshighway & Lindell Boulevard hosted a New Year's Eve party. Management announced the importance of following the law, but the floor-length tablecloths made it easy to hide the alcohol. At 1:30 a.m., Gus O. Nations, teetotaler and St. Louis's chief dry agent, strolled into the hotel's Palm Room with five other officers. They checked beneath the tables until a woman screamed, claiming her gown was grabbed by an agent. Her escort punched the officer, causing chaos to ensue. Detective Ed Sullivan accidentally fired a shot into the floor, grazing three dancers. A former federal judge who attended the party, Henry S. Priest, sued Nations on behalf of one of the wounded dancers. Ten days later, Priest led the Missouri Association Against the Prohibition Amendment with a rally attended by 2,000 people. He battled Prohibition until 1930, when he died three years before repeal.

In 1910, when Tennessee went dry by state law, the Jack Daniel distillery moved to St. Louis. During the onset of national Prohibition, the Jack Daniel plant at 3960 Duncan Avenue held nearly 900 barrels of whiskey. In 1923, despite the warehouse being guarded by federal inspectors, well-connected crooks methodically siphoned 31,000 gallons to trucks waiting in the alley. They refilled the barrels with vinegar and water, all under the watch of chief guard William Kinney, who had family ties to the Egan's Rats gang. The "whiskey milking case" was born when a visiting inspector tasted the vinegar. In 1925, 23 men were convicted in the scam in a federal trial in Indianapolis. The convicts included several prominent St. Louisans, including a former city circuit clerk, Nat Goldstein, and chief federal revenue agent in St. Louis, Arnold Hellmich. Hellmich was also the man responsible for appointing Kinney as the chief guard of the warehouse. They rented a private railroad car for their trip to the Leavenworth, Kansas, prison. More than 4,000 fans cheered them when the train stopped at Union Station.

In 1924, federal agents destroyed a boxcar full of liquor in west St. Louis County. The boxcar was parked on a sidewalk near Denny Road, now known as Lindbergh Boulevard, and Conway Road.

St. Louisan Charlie Birger led a gang in southern Illinois. His main rivals were the country-boy Shelton brothers: Carl, Earl, and Bernie. A former tourist stop 10 miles east of Marion, IL, called the Shady Rest was Birger's hideout.

In 1926, Birger gangsters shot up the home of the brother of the mayor of West City, Illinois, Joe Adams. Joe Adams was an ally of the Shelton brothers. In retaliation, the Sheltons hired a barnstorming pilot to fly one of their gangsters up in a Curtiss Jenny biplane to drop homemade dynamite bombs over Shady Rest. Only one bomb exploded, and it was ineffective. Birger's men lit up the sky with submachine gunfire, but they missed the plane.

One month later, Birger's gang murdered Adams. Birger was convicted in the murder and was executed by hanging in Benton, IL, in 1928. According to the *Post-Dispatch*, Birger said, "I've shot men in my time, but I never shot one that didn't deserve it."

In 1932, two weeks before Election Day, Democratic candidate Franklin D. Roosevelt spoke at a rally in the St. Louis Coliseum at Jefferson & Washington Avenues. More than

12,000 Democrats filled the arena and 5,000 more crowded the sidewalks. They cheered with jubilation when he called for restoring beer production. They chanted, "We want beer!"

Architectural drawing of the new Coliseum at 2600 Washington Avenue, at the southwest corner of Washington & Jefferson. Designed by Frederick C. Bonsack, the new Coliseum was used as an arena and event location. The 1908 building replaced the St. Louis Exposition and Music Hall and was used until the mid-1930s when it was replaced by Kiel Auditorium. It was condemned by the city in 1953. The Coliseum was the site of the 1916 Democratic National Convention, photograph from the St. Louis Public Library Digital Collections, circa 1910.

Four days before the election, President Herbert Hoover spoke at the Coliseum. Despite the urging from St. Louis Republicans to say a good word about alcohol, Hoover refused. With the Depression at its worst, Roosevelt won a 42-state landslide.

On April 6, happy crowds gathered at Falstaff and Anheuser-Busch breweries as midnight approached. As truckloads moved through the crowds for deliveries to the holders of federal permits to sell beer, August A. "Gussie" Busch shouted, "Come and get it." One of the lucky permit holders was the Elks Club at 3619 Lindell Boulevard. There, Mayor-elect Bernard Dickmann led the first round.

On April 7, the first day to celebrate the return of legal beer, more than 600 people attended a party at the Hotel Jefferson, located at what is now Tucker Boulevard & Locust Street.

12th Street (later Tucker Boulevard), St. Louis, "looking south from St. Charles Street, showing some of the most prominent buildings in the city, Post-Dispatch, Star, Union, Electric Light & Power Co. and the Jefferson Hotel, one of the largest and most modern hotels in the city," photograph from the St. Louis Public Library Digital Collections, circa 1910.

On December 5, the 21st Amendment for repeal became part of the U.S. Constitution. The state of Missouri took a while longer to enact their own repeal. When a liquor-store owner was arrested, St. Louis Circuit Attorney Harry Roseman refused to prosecute. Roseman said, "this man has committed no crime."

Source: Tim O'Neil / *St. Louis Post-Dispatch*, April 7, 2021

1918 Washington University Football Team

In 1918, society was dealing with a Spanish flu pandemic and a World War. The Washington University football team, dealt a blow from sickness and the loss of soldiers overseas, was reinforced by students on campus from the Student Army

Training Corps. The Student Army Training Corps (SATC) allowed freshmen or previous college graduates to play football. The SATC students attended classes while training for the military. According to a *Post-Dispatch* article, "Football is THE game for military training, since it develops the head, the heart, the lungs, the legs, a fine sense of obedience and an amenability to discipline."

The team featured the Cleveland Indians' third baseman, Joe Evans, and the former quarterback for the University of Wisconsin, Eber Simpson. Washington University, led by Coach Dick Rutherford, finished undefeated at 6–0 and claimed a conference championship. Because of this unique roster and jumbled schedule, the conference refused to award Washington University with the official championship.

The Washington University Pikers played in the Missouri Valley Conference with Mizzou, Kansas, Drake, and Nebraska. Many Pikers' games were canceled due to St. Louis being quarantined. Fall camp was a struggle as several players had side effects from receiving injections. The team kept practicing and played its first game at Westminster College in Fulton. The team held its first home game on November 2 without any fans.

In November, both the war and the quarantine ended. The city was buzzing about both the "city championship" against Saint Louis University and an upcoming visit from the Nebraska Cornhuskers. The Turkey Day game versus SLU was even more of a spectacle because it gave once-quarantined St. Louisans something to celebrate. Tickets to Washington University's Francis Field were $1.50 for the grandstand box seats. The 19–0 victory over SLU was attended by 7,000 fans.

Despite the conference's refusal to recognize a champion, Nebraska agreed to sanction their match as a championship game. The game brought a lot of hype, and the newspaper even featured photographs on the front of the Sports page, which was rare at the time. Nebraska's front line, feared by many teams, averaged a "whopping" 200 pounds per player. For the December 7 game, grandstand ticket prices rose to $1.65. More than 7,000 fans packed the stadium to witness a 20–7 Washington University victory. After the game, the Nebraska coach described Eber Simpson as "the greatest player I've ever had the good fortune to see."

Joe Evans, who won the World Series with the Cleveland Indians in 1920, became known as "Doc" Evans. He earned the new nickname since he continued to study at Washington University in the off-season and eventually earned his medical degree.

Source: Benjamin Hochman / *St. Louis Post-Dispatch*, April 16, 2020

Babe Ruth's Last Trip to a Big League Park

Most people believe George Herman Ruth's final appearance at a big-league ballpark was on June 13, 1948, when he visited Yankee Stadium for the last time. He wore a full uniform and stood near home plate while leaning on a bat. But on June 19, 1948, Ruth made his actual final appearance at a big-league ballpark when he visited Sportsman's Park in St. Louis and met six-year-old Bill DeWitt Jr., the current Cardinals chairman.

Ruth was diagnosed with throat cancer at age 53. But he still went on a tour of ballparks to promote American Legion Baseball. The tour was sponsored by Ford Motor Company.

Posters around town promoted the big free event. Per the *Post-Dispatch*, 10,120 kids attended the 10:00 a.m. event. Ruth spoke to the kids, but due to his throat condition, it was difficult to understand him. On the field, he met the six-year-old DeWitt, who was the son of a St. Louis Browns executive.

DeWitt wore a Browns batboy's uniform, the same uniform that was worn three years later by three-foot-seven Eddie Gaedel in his historic lone at bat for the Browns, a four-pitch walk. DeWitt's father had the photographer quickly print the photograph so Ruth could autograph it for his son.

View of North Grand looking north from near Dodier Street. Sportsman's Park is visible on the left side of the image. The Speedway Publishing sign at 3107 - 09 N. Grand is visible in the background, as is the YMCA building at 3106. Igou Motors can be seen on the right. Photograph by Richard W. Lemen, July 25, 1931.

Also that month, Ruth visited Yale and met George H. W. Bush, the baseball team's captain.

Fifty-eight days after his visit to St. Louis, Ruth passed away. Also unique to St. Louis, Ruth had arguably the greatest World Series performance at Sportman's Park in 1926. In one game during the series, he hit three home runs, walked twice, scored four total runs, and tallied an outfield assist. One of his home runs sailed out of the stadium and broke a front window of Wells Motor Co. on North Grand Boulevard.

Source: Benjamin Hochman / *St. Louis Post-Dispatch*, February 6, 2020

William Clark Died in St. Louis

Explorer William Clark named his son, Meriwether Lewis Clark, for his expedition partner and friend. Meriwether would become an architect, engineer, and politician. Meriwether's home was located at what is now Olive & North Broadway.

William Clark died of natural causes at Meriwether's home in 1838 at age 68. Originally, he was buried on his nephew John O'Fallon's property, now known as O'Fallon Park. Clark is now buried at Bellefontaine Cemetery where a 35-foot-tall granite obelisk marks his grave. Several family

William Clark. Portrait, bust, facing right. Illustration by Charles Wilson Peale, circa 1903.

members, including Meriwether, are buried nearby. A plaque at the southeast corner of Broadway & Olive Street notes Clark's death site.

Source: Valerie Schremp Hahn / *St. Louis Post-Dispatch*, April 3 – 9, 2020

Chief Pontiac is Buried in St. Louis

Pontiac, born around 1720, was an Ottowa Indian chief. He had influenced an effort with other tribes to fight the British around the Great Lakes. Possibly in retaliation for an attack, Pontiac was stabbed to death by a Peoria Indian on a visit to the outskirts of Cahokia in 1769. His body was brought across the river and buried in what was then the outskirts of St. Louis. A plaque on the corner of a parking garage at Broadway & Walnut Street marks the location of his gravesite.

Source: Valerie Schremp Hahn / *St. Louis Post-Dispatch*, April 3 – 9, 2020

Pontiac lying on ground; Indian with tomahawk standing over him. Illustration by DeCost Smith, circa 1897.

A Miracle Happened Here

In 1861, German immigrant Ignatius Strecker was hit in the chest by a piece of iron while working at a downtown soap factory. In addition to the constant pain, he was diagnosed with tuberculosis two years after the injury. He was given two weeks to live.

Strecker and his family lived close to St. Joseph's Catholic Church, now known as the Shrine of St. Joseph, at 1220 North 11th Street. A missionary visited to preach about Peter Claver, a 17th-century Jesuit priest. After the missionary laid relics of Claver on Strecker, he was cured and returned to work a few days later. Helped by the miracle at the church, Claver became a saint in 1888.

This event was the only Vatican-sanctioned miracle to happen in St. Louis. Strecker's descendants return to the shrine every March to celebrate. Relics of Claver remain inside the church. A sign outside the church notes it as the site of the miracle.

Source: Valerie Schremp Hahn / *St. Louis Post-Dispatch*, April 3 – 9, 2020

Left: View of North 10th St. & Biddle. Shrine of St. Joseph spire can be seen in background. Photograph by Richard W. Lemen, circa 1930. Right: 931 North 11th Street. View looking north of a man standing in the doorway at Larsson Auto Repair at 931 North 11th Street near the intersection of Washington Boulevard. Catty-corner at 1000 North Eleventh, Anton Riggio's Grocery store is visible. One of the elaborate twin towers of the Shrine of St. Joseph is seen in the distance. Major street work is underway. Photograph by Richard W. Lemen, circa 1930.

St. Louis's Most Historic Hotel?

The current site of the 21-story Gateway Tower at 1 Memorial Drive was once a hotel where Abraham Lincoln, Daniel Webster, Robert E. Lee, Jefferson Davis, and Zachary Taylor all slept. Lincoln was an Illinois congressman at the time and was on his way to Washington, DC. They traveled from Springfield, IL, and boarded a steamboat in St. Louis.

Originally built in the 1830s as Scott's Hotel, the structure had several other names, including the luxury National Hotel. The hotel burned down and was rebuilt in 1847 then was finally demolished in 1948. A plaque was placed on the current building in 1974 noting that Lincoln, his wife Mary, their young sons Tad and Edward, and friend Joshua Speed slept at Scott's Hotel in 1846.

Old National Hotel, Third & National Streets, St. Louis. Photograph from the Historic American Buildings Survey collection of the Library of Congress Prints and Photographs Division.

Erastus Wells, the namesake of Wellston, established the city's first bus route in 1843 when he hitched two horses to an old Army ambulance wagon and drove it from Scott's Hotel to the ferry landing at North Market Street.

Another plaque on the current structure notes it as the birthplace of KMOX radio in 1925 and where young guitarist Les Paul first worked, using the nickname "Rhubarb Red."

Source: Valerie Schremp Hahn / *St. Louis Post-Dispatch*, April 3 – 9, 2020

Plaque on the New National Hotel, 300 Market Street, near the north elevation of the St. Louis riverfront. Photograph by Theodore LaVack, June 23, 1936.

The American Legion Was Born Here

A plaque noting the spot where the St. Louis caucus of the American Legion met in 1919 to draw up its first constitution was placed in 2009. The plaque is located at the former Schubert Theatre at 301 North Tucker Boulevard, now a U.S. Bank branch. The Theater was located inside the Union Pacific building.

The building once also had a plaque, placed in 1935, noting it as the American Legion's birthplace. The building was eventually demolished. The old plaque was moved to a monument, erected in 1942, at Eternal Flame Park near Soldiers Memorial.

Source: Valerie Schremp Hahn / *St. Louis Post-Dispatch*, April 3 – 9, 2020

Soldiers Memorial, 1315 Chestnut Street, St. Louis, was dedicated on Memorial Day 1938. The architectural firm was Mauran, Russell & Crowell. On opposite side: "Published by Gibson Merchandise Co., St. Louis," and "Photograph courtesy St. Louis Chamber of Commerce." Circa 1940.

The First Missouri Legislature

On September 18, 1820, the state's first legislature met at the Missouri Hotel, which stood on what is now known as Laclede's Landing. Alexander McNair, Missouri's first governor, was inaugurated the next day. David Barton and Thomas Hart Benton were elected as the state's first United States senators by the assembly a couple weeks later. The assembly also created 10 new counties and chose St. Charles as the location of the state's first capital.

Left: Thomas Hart Benton, 1782 – 1858. Half length, facing left. Photograph from the Library of Congress Prints and Photographs Division, circa 1858. Right: The statue of Missouri Senator Thomas Hart Benton by Harriet Goodhue Hosmer is located in Lafayette Park, St. Louis. Originally dedicated in 1868, it was recently restored and rededicated in 2011. Photograph from the St. Louis Public Library Digital Collections, circa 1910.

According to *A History of Missouri*, Rep. Daniel Ralls was ill and near death during the convening of the legislature. The legislature had him and his bed carried downstairs to cast a deciding vote for Benton, who won the seat. Shortly after Ralls returned to his room, he died. The legislature named one of the new counties for Ralls.

A plaque marking this spot is just to the right of the Old Spaghetti Factory entrance at Morgan & First streets. The current building, one of the country's largest cast-iron-front buildings, was built in 1874 as the home for the Christian Peper Tobacco Co.

Source: Valerie Schremp Hahn / *St. Louis Post-Dispatch*, April 3 – 9, 2020

A sketch of the Missouri Hotel, which was begun in 1817, finished in 1819, and opened in 1820, by David Massey. It was located at the southwest corner of Main & Oak (later Morgan) Streets, St. Louis. The hotel was the site of the first state legislature, which met on September 8, 1820. After 1821, Major Thomas Biddle built an addition on the hotel.

View of west elevation (front) of the First State Legislative Assembly Hall, 208 – 214 South Main Street, Saint Charles. Photograph by George Harkness III, April 10, 1934.

Planter's Punch

Around 1840, a bartender at the Planter's House hotel, Kerry Thomas, mixed rum, lemon juice, and orange juice to create the Planter's Punch cocktail. The Planter's House hotel stood on Fourth Street between Chestnut and Pine from 1817 until 1922. Abraham Lincoln, Jefferson Davis, Andrew Jackson, Henry Clay, Ulysses S. Grant, and William B. "Buffalo Bill" Cody all slept there. In 1841, Charles Dickens stayed there and gave it a raving review.

Planters Hotel, St. Louis, circa 1901. photograph from the Detroit Publishing Company Photograph Collection of the Library of Congress Prints and Photographs Division,

The location is now the Bank of America tower. A plaque marking the location of the hotel can be seen on a low wall on Fourth Street. The present-day Planter's House is a cocktail bar and restaurant named after the historic hotel. There you can order the Planter's House Punch.

Source: Valerie Schremp Hahn / *St. Louis Post-Dispatch*, April 3 – 9, 2020

Washington University

Washington University was founded in 1853, first known as Eliot Seminary. In 1856, it moved inside a three-story building called Academic Hall at Washington Avenue & 17th Street. Due to the population increase downtown in the 1890s and nearby saloons and gambling dens, the school's chancellor decided to acquire a tract of land just west of Skinker Boulevard. In 1900, the new campus's first building, Adolphus Busch Hall, was laid. A plaque marks the location of the first campus on the southwest corner of Washington & 17th.

Source: Valerie Schremp Hahn / *St. Louis Post-Dispatch*, April 3 – 9, 2020

Washington University leased its University Hall to the Louisiana Purchase Exposition Company to be used as the fair's Administration building. After the fair, the university renamed the building Brookings Hall. Photograph from the Louisiana Purchase Exposition Glass Plate Negatives collection of the St. Louis Public Library, circa 1902.

Busch Hall, one of the buildings leased from Washington University for the Louisiana Purchase Exposition, was used by the Louisiana Purchase Exposition's Department of Works' architects and engineers. After the fair, it housed the university's chemistry department. Photograph from the Louisiana Purchase Exposition Glass Plate Negatives collection of the St. Louis Public Library, circa 1902.

Private Streets in St. Louis

The advent of private streets in St. Louis began before the Civil War. In 1851, Lucas Place was developed near downtown. The development is commemorated by the Campbell House Museum at 1508 Locust Street, the lone remaining structure from Lucas Place.

The Campbell House Museum, 15th & Locust, in downtown St. Louis. This image is from a Topic-color production by Argro Foto & Postcard Co., St. Louis and reads: "The former home of Robert Campbell, wealthy fur trader of mid 1800's, [sic] now open to the public. The home is lavishly furnished with most of the original Campbell belongings including furniture of the ante-bellum era. The carriage house, summer house and front fence of cast iron remain as the Campbells left them." Photograph by Art Grossman, circa 1964.

Surveyor Julius Pitzman championed the idea to develop residences along parklike streets where traffic could be restricted. These streets would be maintained by the residents. Prior to zoning regulations, the private streets had strict guidelines regarding the size of the lots and the design of the homes. The city's population nearly doubled between 1860 and 1870. With this population growth, wealthier St. Louisans found their neighborhoods being surrounded by commercial and industrial businesses, increasing the demand of private streets.

After the Civil War, Pitzman laid out Benton Place near Lafayette Square and Vandeventer Place, where the John Cochran Veterans Hospital stands now north of downtown. By the late 1870s, several of the city's most powerful and wealthy residents were living in the mansions on Vandeventer and Benton Places.

St. Louis continued to expand farther west, and when it was announced that Forest Park would host a World's Fair, Pitzman decided to create new private streets. Laid out in 1888, Portland and Westmoreland Places are located just north of Lindell Boulevard and Forest Park. The first homes opened in 1890. Both streets are now listed on the National Register of Historic Places. Due to so many powerful people living on these two streets, they were uniquely self-sufficient. According to Julius Hunter, author of *Westmoreland and Portland Places*, everything needed to purchase and equip a new residence, including bank loans, bricks, stone, glass, electricity, gas, and appliances, could be obtained from a company headed by a neighbor.

Source: Joe Holleman / *St. Louis Post-Dispatch*, June 30, 2020

Left: Private streets, such as Washington Terrace, were developed in St. Louis in the late 19th century. Julius Pitzman laid out the street with 50 lots. Harvey Ellis and architect George R. Mann designed the entrance gates. Circa 1900. Right: View of Westmoreland Place, a private street in St. Louis, shows a number of its stately homes. On opposite side: "Adolph Selige Publishing Co., St. Louis. Made in Germany." Circa 1910.

Remaining 1904 World's Fair Structures

All photographs in this section are from the Louisiana Purchase Exposition Glass Plate Negatives collection of the St. Louis Public Library unless otherwise noted.

Flight cage at the Saint Louis Zoo

Erecting the United States Bird Cage for the 1904 World's Fair. In early 1904, men work on construction of the U.S. Bird Cage exhibit for the Louisiana Purchase Exposition while others look on. The Smithsonian Institution built the Bird Cage to display birds in a natural environment. The Bird Cage remained in Forest Park as part of the Saint Louis Zoo. Photograph dated April 1904.

Saint Louis Art Museum

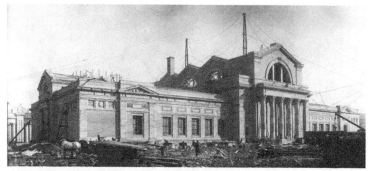

A view of the construction of architect Cass Gilbert's Palace of Fine Arts for the Louisiana Purchase Exposition. It was one of the exposition's few permanent buildings remaining after the World's Fair as the Saint Louis Art Museum. Photograph dated January 7, 1904.

A recast statue of St. Louis's namesake, French King Louis IX, known as the "Apotheosis of St. Louis."

The Apotheosis of St. Louis, the equestrian statue of Louis IX, King of France and patron saint of the city of St. Louis, was situated at the Plaza of St. Louis at the Louisiana Purchase Exposition (1904 World's Fair). Constructed by sculptor Charles H. Niehaus of reinforced plaster for the exposition, it later was cast in bronze and placed on Art Hill in Forest Park before the Saint Louis Art Museum. Photograph by Jessie Tarbox Beals, May 1904.

The clockwork from the fair's Great Floral Clock is located inside the Missouri History Museum.

Building the Floral Clock for the 1904 World's Fair. Workmen with the assistance of mules set up the mechanisms for the giant Floral Clock in the area north of the Palace of Agriculture at the Louisiana Purchase Exposition. A working clock decorated with red coleus, its dials measured 112 feet in diameter; each hand weighed 2,500 pounds; its numerals were 15 feet high. Mechanisms for the floral clock were supplied by the Department of Manufactures; a 5,000-lb. bell in the structure on the right struck on the hour and half hour; an hourglass was placed in the left structure. The popular attraction was illuminated at night. Photograph dated April 28, 1904.

A bird's eye view of the Palace of Agriculture and the Ceylon and Canada pavilions for the Louisiana Purchase Exposition (1904 World's Fair). The outline for placement of the Floral Clock can be seen in front of the Agriculture palace. Photograph dated February 24, 1904.

*The main stadium for the 1904 Olympic Games at Washington
University's Francis Field.*

Building the stadium for the 1904 World's Fair. A view of the west end of the
stadium under construction. The first concrete stadium in the United States
was built for the Louisiana Purchase Exposition. The athletic site remains as
Washington University's Francis Field. Photograph dated January 9, 1904.

*The American Radiator Building is located on Kenilworth Place in
Webster Groves.*

At the exhibit in the Palace of Manufactures. The American Radiator Company,
Chicago, showed its heating apparatus in a cutaway full-size house. Note
the fence around the exhibit made of radiators. After the fair, the house was
moved by rail to Webster Groves. With a new front and kitchen, it remains as
a residence on Kenilworth Place. Photograph published in 1905.

The Nevada Pavilion is located on Schultz Road in Oakland.

The Nevada building at the Louisiana Purchase Exposition (1904 World's Fair). Photograph dated April 22, 1904.

The West Virginia building is located on East Monroe Avenue in Oakland.

Architects Giesly & Harris of Wheeling designed the West Virginia Pavilion for the Louisiana Purchase Exposition (1904 World's Fair) as a colonial style building. Photograph dated March 8, 1904.

The French colonial Cahokia Courthouse was rebuilt for permanent display in Cahokia.

A replica of the Old Cahokia Court House was part of the Old St. Louis concession on the Pike at the Louisiana Purchase Exposition (1904 World's Fair). The concession reproduced St. Louis and historic regional buildings as they stood in 1764. Photograph dated April 18, 1904.

General Grant's Cabin sits on the grounds of Grant's Farm.

Ulysses S. Grant's St. Louis County farm building was exhibited at the Louisiana Purchase Exposition (1904 World's Fair). Cyrus F. Blanke, president of the C. F. Blanke Tea & Coffee Co. and director of the Louisiana Purchase Exposition Company, had recently purchased the cabin. Photograph dated March 30, 1904.

Grant Road log cabin, Affton, St. Louis County. Photograph from the Historic American Buildings Survey collection of the Library of Congress Prints and Photographs Division, compiled after 1933.

A statue called Forest Devotion, which was originally displayed at the fair's Palace of Varied Industries, is now the grave marker for August A. Busch Sr. in Sunset Memorial Park in St. Louis County.

Entrance to the Palace of Varied Industries at the Louisiana Purchase Exposition (1904 World's Fair). Photograph dated 1904.

Source: Colter Peterson / *St. Louis Post-Dispatch*, March 25, 2020

Forest Park Horse Stables

A long barn provides shelter for four horses in the St. Louis Metropolitan Police Department's mounted unit in the southeast quadrant of Forest Park. But prior to that, it housed airplanes.

After World War I, the United States Postal Service set up the first coast-to-coast airmail route. The route stretched from New York to San Francisco, passing through Chicago. The St. Louis postmaster proposed creating a route that extended from Chicago to St. Louis. City Hall and the Chamber of Commerce each paid $12,500 to build a hangar and a runway, clearing about 100 acres of Forest Park in the process.

On August 16, 1920, the first airmail flight took off from the park, transporting roughly 150 pounds of mail. On average, the planes delivered letters to Chicago in under four hours, as compared to the eight hours it took by train.

The Forest Park airmail service lasted less than a year, closing on June 30, 1921. Congress failed to appropriate the funding needed to keep the service going. The aircraft had carried 52,000 pounds of mail.

After the airmail service ceased operations, Robertson Aircraft Corporation, a private firm, used the Forest Park airfield. The company bought a Curtiss JN-4 Jenny biplane left over from the war. The business offered flight lessons and sightseeing flights. For $20 a day, Ralston Purina hired the company to paint the checkerboard logo on their plane and drop advertisements onto farm property.

After residents who lived near Forest Park complained about the noise, Robertson Aircraft Corporation relocated to the area that is now St. Louis Lambert International Airport.

The Boeing Aviation Fields, featuring four baseball and four softball fields, are now located in the area in Forest Park that used to be the airfield. In the 1970s, the St. Louis Metropolitan Police Department's mounted unit moved into the hangar. Forest Park Forever raised $900,000 for a renovation after lead paint was discovered in the hangar in 2009. In 2013, the unit returned to the hangar and remains there today.

Source: *St. Louis Magazine*, August 2020

Random Bits

⨝ Plymouth Rock hens from Kirkwood won the blue ribbon in the poultry exhibit at the Panama-Pacific International Exhibition in San Francisco in 1915.

Panama-Pacific International Exposition. Photograph by James David Givens, circa 1915.

View of the Panama-Pacific International Exposition grounds. Photograph by H. S. Crocker & Co., circa 1914.

◁ When St. Louisan Cory Smith drove his St. Louis car, a 1910 Dorris, out west in 1915 to see the Panama-Pacific International Exhibition in San Francisco, he made history as a part of the first big wave of people to take a "road trip." He was answering the fair's call to "See America First."

◁ Warsaw, MO, is the site of the state's hottest-ever day (118 degrees in July 1954) and its coldest-ever day (minus 40 degrees in February 1905).

◁ Chillicothe, MO, is home to America's first sliced-bread bakery.

◁ St. Louis is the only major city outside of the Great Lakes region that participates in the Northern Cities Shift in which short vowel sounds drift into other vowels' territory. One prominent example of this is that many Missourians pronounce the state's name as *Missour-ah* or *Missour-uh* rather than *Missour-ee*. St. Louisans also notoriously — and hilariously, to some — tend to pronounce the name of Highway 40 as "farty" and Highway 44 as "farty far."

Sources: Stefene Russell / *St. Louis Magazine*, August 2020; *St. Louis Post-Dispatch*, March 15, 2020; Harry Levins / *St. Louis Post-Dispatch*, June 12, 2020

Floral Clock outside the Palace of Agriculture. The Floral Clock at the Louisiana Purchase Exposition (1904 World's Fair) was a working clock decorated with red coleus. Its dials measured 112 feet in diameter; each hand weighed 2,500 pounds; its numerals were 15 feet high. The popular attraction was illuminated at night. Mechanisms for the floral clock were supplied by the Department of Manufactures. The small house contained mechanisms for the clock. A 5,000 lb. bell to the right of the house struck on hour and half hour; the hourglass sat in the left structure. Photograph dated 1904. See page 228.

ABOUT THE AUTHOR

My name is Michael Kleckner. I was born and raised in St. Louis County. In 2009, I graduated from the Journalism School at the University of Missouri–Columbia.

I have lived in Kirkwood since 2011 with my wife, Christine; son, Teddy; daughter, Josie; dog, Lucy; and two cats, Truman and Jack.

For all of my adult life, I have been extremely passionate about St. Louis history. I love touring the beautiful mansions in the Central West End. I have read nearly every St. Louis and Missouri history book available. Going to a local park begins with a brisk walk for exercise and turns into me spending hours researching what that monument off in the distance represents. I may come across the name of an early settler in a book about Town & Country history, then I want to know everything about that individual. Who were his children? Besides owning land, with what else was he involved? What areas of town, subdivisions, or streets are named after him? My wife can't go to the Missouri Botanical Garden without me telling her all about Henry Shaw. A perfect day for me could involve driving around Florissant with my mom to explore the parts of town in which my family lived prior to me being born.

I am also an avid reader. I read EVERYTHING. Magazines, newspapers, newsletters, flyers, brochures, etc. This includes everything from *West Newsmagazine and the Webster-Kirkwood Times to the Chesterfield Out & About magazine and the Town & Country newsletter.*

My passion for St. Louis and love for reading combined with my curious nature resulted in the creation of this book.

Thank you to my mother (also an avid reader), Robin Snitzer, for saving me every publication she reads and for buying me nearly every St. Louis history book for birthdays and Christmas. Thank you to my wife for putting up with me and acting like she is interested in my unprompted, unprovoked St. Louis history tours whenever we go anywhere. One day I will give her a date night that doesn't involve me telling her that the restaurant at which we are dining is in a registered historic building.

iNDEX

Note: Page numbers in *italics* indicate photographs and drawings.

Made in the USA
Coppell, TX
08 December 2021

67561919R00152